S0-BLW-046

Culture and Space

Culture and Space

Conceiving a new cultural geography

Joël Bonnemaison

Edited by Chantal Blanc-Pamard,
Maud Lasseur and Christel Thibault

Translated by Josée Pénot-Demetry

I.B. TAURIS
LONDON · NEW YORK

ïi institut français

This book is supported by the French Ministry for Foreign Affairs, as part of the Burgess programme headed for the French Embassy in London by the Institut Français du Royaume-Uni.

First published in French as *La géographie culturelle* by Éditions du CTHS © CTHS 2000, 2004

This English translation first published in 2005
by I.B. Tauris & Co. Ltd
6 Salem Road, London W2 4BU
175 Fifth Avenue, New York NY 10010
Website www.ibtauris.com

In the United States of America and Canada distributed by
Palgrave Macmillan, a division of St Martin's Press
175 Fifth Avenue, New York NY 10010

Introduction copyright © John Agnew 2005
This translation copyright © Josée Pénot-Demetry 2005

International Library of Human Geography 8

ISBN 1 86064 908 4 pbk
ISBN 1 86064 907 6 hbk

EAN 978 1 86064 908 0 pbk
EAN 978 1 86064 907 3 hbk

A full CIP record for this book is available from the British Library

Library of Congress catalog card: available

Typeset in Garamond by JCS Publishing Services
Printed and bound in Great Britain by TJ International Ltd, Padstow, Cornwall

Contents

List of illustrations

Preface to the French edition

This book presents a series of university lectures by geographer Joël Bonnemaison, a researcher at ORSTOM who, in 1994, became professor at the University of Paris Sorbonne (Paris IV). In July 1997, Bonnemaison died suddenly while on a research mission in New Caledonia. Two of his students, Maud Lasseur and Christel Thibault, have been instrumental in making his lectures known to a larger public as they, along with fellow students Lydie Laberrondo and Laure Michel, compiled their coursework notes on which this book is based. All four students had been attending undergraduate and graduate classes at the Institute of Geography in 1994–97.

Joël Bonnemaison's goal was to 'explore the new paths of cultural geography'. Through teaching, he also wished to share his ongoing analysis of the cultural foundations of human geography. His course was based on files and personal notes; Martine Bonnemaison, his wife, gathered these after his death. These documents were compared with the students' notes. With unfailing determination and enthusiasm, all documents were thoroughly cross-checked and assembled into the present text. We did not make any editing changes as this would have encroached upon the author's role and misrepresented the following text, which is, first of all, a testimony.

In the small amphitheatre at the Institute of Geography, Joël Bonnemaison taught with verve, passion, and humour. Speaking with conviction and persuasion, sprinkling his lectures with numerous examples, he knew how to captivate his audience. An echo of that richness and enthusiasm lingers in this somewhat austere compilation, which we tried to design with the utmost precision and care. These lectures are now far removed from the unforgettable moments when they were delivered, therefore we have added excerpts from Bonnemaison's articles and books to illustrate some of his favourite themes and to pay homage to his writing style.

Joël Bonnemaison was not able to read these notes, and neither did he have the time to complete the book that he had planned to write on the basis of his lectures at the Sorbonne. We hope that we have shown respect to Bonnemaison's memory and that, thanks to the present publication by CTHS (Committee for Historical and Scientific Works), of which he was a member, the work of his students will contribute to keeping his thought alive.

Augustin Berque and Chantal Blanc-Pamard
Sendai and Paris, March 2000

Translator's acknowledgements

Special thanks are due to Chantal Blanc-Pamard, John A. Agnew and Denis Cosgrove for their interest in this project and their help in finding a publisher. I am grateful to David Stonestreet, geography editor at I.B. Tauris, for his confidence and support. The publishing of this book is a sign of pluralism in an era of globalization.

The translation has benefited from the tremendous detective work of Chantal Blanc-Pamard, Martine Bonnemaison, Philippe Couty, Alain Gascon, Christian Huetz de Lemps, Maud Lasseur, Jean-Claude Rivierre and Christel Thibault in France, and R. Gerard Ward and Darrell Tryon in Australia, who cross-checked references and quotations under severe time constraints. As this project demonstrated, the old Bonnemaison network is well and alive. Ben L. Weinberg, Jr. reviewed the text, and I am grateful for his suggestions.

Introduction to the English edition

John Agnew (UCLA)

Cultural differences can only be adequately understood when placed in their geographical context. This is the basic premise of Joël Bonnemaison's approach to cultural geography, translated here from the original French under the title *Culture and Space*. Along with Paul Claval, who is much better known than Bonnemaison in the English-speaking world, he has been the main advocate of a French school of cultural geography or, more accurately in Bonnemaison's case, a human geography intensely invested in exploring cultural differences in spatial sensibility. His perspective on culture and space is based on a long and productive career as a geographical field worker, first in Madagascar and later in the Melanesian (western Pacific) islands of Vanuatu and New Caledonia. Dying at the relatively young age of 57 while on a field trip to New Caledonia in 1997, Bonnemaison had intended to publish a book laying out his general approach to 'cultural geography'. Tragically, this did not come to pass. The present volume consists of students' notes taken in his lectures at the University of Paris IV (the Sorbonne) and of excerpts from published sources – mainly examples of cultural practices and geosymbolism in Vanuatu, where Bonnemaison undertook most of his best known fieldwork – in an effort to provide something of the general statement about his philosophy of cultural geography that he was not able to do for himself. It also includes a bibliography of the writings of Joël Bonnemaison for benefit of those who would like to pursue in greater detail themes raised in this book.

This book is appearing in English translation for a number of reasons, all of which speak to the theoretical originality and passion for empirical fieldwork that characterize the research and writing of Joël Bonnemaison. For one thing, if cultural geography in the English-speaking world has become largely an armchair pursuit, partly out of a real fear that Western observers will bear false witness to the voices of others but also because of a confusion that engaging in empirical research necessarily entails an atheoretical empiricism, Bonnemaison's approach is a salutary reminder that neither of these need prove immobilizing. Famous for the precision of his fieldwork (see, e.g. Philibert and Rodman 1998, 100), Bonnemaison took considerable care with his theoretical exposition as well. But his approach also represents a sophisticated case for the idea that cultural differences are produced in cultural exchange at a variety of geographical scales and are not simply the result of 'bunkered', essentialized or rigidly bounded cultures that exist independent of time and place and 'zap' their members into conformity. In other words, cultures are not simply unchanging traditions inherited wholesale from the past. Thus, in this construction it is fatuous to think, after centuries of European colonialism, that there are pure or uncontaminated cultures or that there have been many such pristine entities for time immemorial. Yet, there are significant cultural differences between places. The task of cultural geography is to elucidate these and show, as far as possible, how they come about and operate.

Perhaps most importantly, however, Bonnemaison's approach to cultural geography is inherently geographical at a time in the English-speaking world when cultural geography often seems indistinguishable from a larger field of cultural studies in which space and place hardly figure at all except metaphorically. He extends the classic understanding of the sacred, for example, from the social role of sacralization in itself to the *geography* of symbolization and social communication that it performs at the core of a culture. Rituals, for example, involving religious, social and political rites and myths that sacralize things, people and events in particular networks of places provide a window onto how the larger culture, as opposed to society and religion per se, is organized. To Bonnemaison, therefore, it is the spatial sensibilities of different groups that are at the root of their cultural differences. Thus, in the examples he draws from his fieldwork in Melanesia, Bonnemaison shows how 'geosymbols' are at the heart of the everyday lives of people who after an earlier flirtation with missionary Christianity have elaborated a syncretic belief system that is known by the label '*kastom*' (or custom). Their reliance on reticulated (networked) space, or places drawn together by their symbolic significance, contrasts with the hierarchical organization of space associated with state-based Western territoriality and spatial networks. Globalization, as Bonnemaison noted, entails a movement towards a more networked global space and away from rigid territoriality. But the networks of globalization are intensely hierarchical, reaching back to central controlling nodes in such places as Paris, New York and Washington DC. Bonnemaison's book, *The Tree and the Canoe: History and Ethnogeography of Tanna* (1994), is well worth consulting as follow-up reading on the contrasting spatial sensibilities of *kastom* supporters on one side and nation-builders (influenced by the '*skul*', school/church) on the other. But the tree and canoe metaphor is older than the recent 'culture wars' in Tanna: it represents a foundational myth of Tannese society akin to that of Romulus and Remus to the ancient Romans. If 'tree' stands for rootedness in place, then 'canoe' represents disruption and movement. In this perspective, Bonnemaison understands culture as the necessary, if contested and fragile, outcome of both.

Finally, Bonnemaison's cultural geography represents a theoretical outlook that, while certainly informed by the history of and trends in English-language cultural geography, is definitely distinctive. It is first and foremost an ethnogeography, methodologically closer to ethnology and cultural anthropology than to much contemporary anglophone cultural geography. In this respect Bonnemaison shares more in common, say, with the essayists in Akhil Gupta and James Ferguson (1997) *Culture, Power, Place: Explorations in Critical Anthropology* than much of what is written in such journals as *Cultural Geographies* (formerly *Ecumene*) or *Society and Space* or most of the cultural geographies celebrated in the recent *Handbook of Cultural Geography* (Anderson et al. 2003). To the extent that I would see a theoretical affinity between Bonnemaison's approach and that of anglophone geographers, it is an affinity to geographers such as Robert Sack (1997, 2003), Yi-Fu Tuan (1977), Doreen Massey (1999), Nicholas Entrikin (1991) and myself (Agnew 2002), who try to balance human rootedness in place with pressures – such as migration, colonialism, investment and trade – that disrupt and reorganize places. Given his predilection for empirical fieldwork, however, Bonnemaison might find much of this writing too abstract and missing the concrete connections to real people and places which his cultural geography necessarily privileges. Also of importance in situating his theoretical outlook, and paralleling a trend in some English-language works, according to Louis Dupont, the Quebec geographer (1998, 107), Bonnemaison said to him that 'Cultural geography, political geography, it's the same thing', implying that questions of political power and identity (including the future of Quebecois and French identities) are central to Bonnemaison's version of cultural geography. This emphasis certainly shows through in his writings about Vanuatu, particularly the close attention he gives to conflicts between different political movements. Of course, his approach also draws significantly on the French tradition in human geography. This tradition, with its roots in the writings of Paul Vidal de la Blache in the early twentieth century, still has much to offer to a wider international audience, not least in its focus on human agency and historical contingency in the making of human cultures as ensembles of beliefs, rituals and practices. These elements are largely foreign to much contemporary anglophone cultural geography, which is often engaged in seemingly endless philosophical disputes, and ironically draws much on glosses of French philosopher-intellectuals such as Althusser, Derrida, Foucault and Lacan, to name just four, over whether culture is fundamental or superstructural (determined by economic processes) (see, e.g. Mitchell 1995) or whether culture exists at all except in the minds of those who refer to it (see, e.g. Duncan and Ley 1993). 'Old Europe', therefore, represented here by a Gascon Frenchman who spent large parts of his life abroad but who never forgot about the local place he was from, still has much 'new' to offer in counterpoint to those in anglophone geography determined to see the world in either purely economic or entirely idealist terms. Yes, there are alternatives to such polarized thinking!

I met Joël Bonnemaison only once, at a conference on regionalist political movements organized by Paul Claval at Étampes, south of Paris, in June 1984, although I did carry on a correspondence with him for some time thereafter. He was immensely friendly and engaging, yet also doggedly committed to the theoretical perspective he was developing from his research. We talked at length about the cultural peculiarities of islands, their roles as crossroads and their vulnerability to external powers. We also discussed the impact of missionaries on island cultures. Knowing of his own research on the impact of Scottish Reformed Presbyterian Church missionaries – a particularly dour and strict Protestant sect that had broken with the established Church of Scotland – on Vanuatu, I told him that the islands of the Inner and Outer Hebrides of Scotland had also been missionized by Calvinists from the Scottish lowlands in the late eighteenth and early nineteenth centuries, if rather more successfully from the viewpoint of the missionaries than in Vanuatu (known until the 1980s by their colonial name 'The New Hebrides'!) After the conference I sent Joël a copy of a rather notorious Scottish novel by Fionn MacColla, *And the Cock Crew*, about the impact of Presbyterianism on the old Gaelic culture of northwestern Scotland. The novel revolves around an opposition remarkably similar to that of *kastom* and *skul* in Vanuatu. This is that between Fearchar, the Gaelic poet, who speaks for tradition and continuity, and Maighstir Sachairi, the minister, who heralds a more modern world of control, submission and absolute necessity. As with Bonnemaison, MacColla finds the seeds of social change and continuity not in simple economic causes but in the commitments and agency of 'the human heart'.

Indeed, Bonnemaison thought of places or territories (as he would call them) in profoundly emotional terms. One could say that much of his work in the 1980s and 1990s was taken up with exploring the emotional attachments to and detachments from place. *The Tree and the Canoe* is a pioneering essay in the geography of emotions, intent on deciphering the 'geographical feelings' and 'places of the heart' that animate the Tannese understanding of their place in the world. A recent trend in the biology of cognition and neuroscience suggests that emotions are critical to cognition rather than in opposition to them as the Cartesian view, long dominant in the social sciences, would suppose (e.g. Damasio 2003). Perhaps Bonnemaison, therefore, was ahead of his time in ascribing cognitive significance to the emotional dimension of culturally mediated spatial sensibilities.

The present volume cannot be taken to be a complete statement of Joël Bonnemaison's cultural geography. It is based on partial sources and has been brought together by others. It is not a typical textbook, in that it does not contain the thoroughly elaborated theoretical arguments or the geographical range of examples that one expects from that genre of publication. What it does do, however, is provide the flavour of the approach that Bonnemaison took to his work and how he might have constructed a more completely worked-out general statement of his position. It also includes sufficient reference to the man himself to see how his career as an indefatigable fieldworker led to the theoretical positions that he adopts in his lecture notes and in the examples introduced from prior publications. A textbook might well be missing this personal undertone. The book also includes much of the nomenclature or specialized vocabulary that Bonnemaison developed as part of his theoretical perspective. Key terms include *reticulated space*, which means a network of spatial links that has no evident centre or periphery; *networked society*, which refers to a society bonded through nodes tied together in a spatial network; *islandness*, meaning the spatial perceptions involved in relating land to sea that come from living on an island; *ante-world*, signifying either a previous social world or a present-day rival or oppositional one, as in *kastom* versus *skul*; *iconology*, referring to the cultural meanings invested in particular landscape features (drawing from the similar usage of Jean Gottmann); and *geosymbol*, meaning the specific association made between a particular spatial location and a cultural belief system.

As it stands, the book does many things successfully but it is also, perhaps inevitably given its origin as a reconstruction of fragments, missing some important clarifications and elaborations. First, to the successes. The organization of the book allows the reader to see how Bonnemaison moved from a critical appreciation of established notions of human and cultural geography in France and elsewhere through an examination of critical concepts such as culture and civilization and the idea of a cultural system to a focus on place or *territory*, as he refers to it in his lectures, as the centrepiece for his cultural geography. As Vincent Berdoulay (1989) has said, French geography has tended to use the term territory analogously to that of place in anglophone usage. In both cases, however, the terms imply a similar emphasis: 'a concern for integration' or a humanistic view of place-making by people and 'the idea of place as a meaningful portion of geographical space' in which 'there is a special, usually emotional link between people and place – the latter understood as a concrete and very specific area' (Berdoulay 1989, 125). In English, the word 'territory' tends to be associated with statehood in one way or another. In French, however, 'territory' is a more concrete rendition of a more abstract 'place'. Bonnemaison preferred to maintain this distinction. In Chapter 2, the pages devoted to German and American (Berkeley school) geography are particularly useful in that they emphasize some of their more positive features at a time in anglophone cultural geography when such past traditions are largely reviled. The examples in the book are testimony to the dynamic conception of culture that pervades Bonnemaison's approach to cultural geography. At the same time that he reports on the foundational location myths and rituals of the Tannese people (from the southernmost island of Tanna in the Vanuatu archipelago), he shows that change is integral to them. They are not static but, as a result of social tumult and population movement, custom is modified into 'a new *kastom* that is partly re-discovered but also partly re-created' in the face of crisis (*The Tree and the Canoe*, 1994, 112). Culture, therefore, is constantly in a process of becoming as a result of discovery, invention, innovation, evolution and diffusion. Bonnemaison's novel understanding of the anthropology of space shines through in these pages. In particular, what the Canadian anthropologists Philibert and Rodman (1998, 100) have said more generally about his research holds true here: 'The power of place to shape and express people's identity was clear in his work on Tanna. But rootedness was only half the story: without movement to provide contrast, rootedness would be meaningless. Mythic movements of stones and heroes on Tanna described paths and intersections, roads and nodes, fundamental to contemporary as well as traditional social organization.' The attention to geographical scale in moving between concepts of culture and civilization is also a major feature of the book, showing how in the contemporary world it is mistaken to think in singular terms with respect to either. The world is not simply 'the West and the Rest', nor is it simply a set of hermetically sealed cultures with distinctive identities set in stone for all time. Cultures and civilizations (or macrocultures) are created in confluence rather than in opposition or in isolation. Bonnemaison's suspicion of historical 'grand narratives' or ideologies that situate places within an overall story also comes through powerfully in this book. Bonnemaison thought that stories such as 'from primitive to modern' both understate the importance of place differences in themselves and miss the openness and unpredictability of human history. For example, the inhabitants of Bonnemaison's beloved Tanna, apparently more sceptical of the first European visitors in the eighteenth century (such as Captain Cook) than the more gullible (hence more 'civilized') Polynesian islanders further east – who are often alleged to have taken the white men for gods, at least in the eyes of the visitors themselves – and because their darker pigmentation and other characteristics marked them as further back along the road to modernity, had consequently acquired the designation of 'savages' from these visitors (for examination of Cook's second voyage in general and the views of the voyage's naturalist, Johann Reinhold Forster, in particular, see Thomas 1996 and Guest 2002). Bonnemaison saw the fallacy of reading cultures in such a way. To him such readings are abstract exercises in cultural classification based on stage-based narratives of cultural development that the European visitors brought with them to the Pacific. Finally, the book is a *hommage* to an inspiring and dedicated geographer whose ideas and work should be exposed to a wider audience. His career path, his bibliography, his lectures and his writings make up the professional Joël Bonnemaison. They are all either provided summarily or hinted at in this small volume. The book is a modest epitaph to someone whose work has inspired many and a guidepost for those who did not know of him but who can now take motivation from what he has left behind.

Of course, there are many things a compilation such as this cannot do adequately. It does not offer a critical review of contemporary anglophone cultural geography. It does not address its own intellectual antecedents in anthropology or where Bonnemaison might differ with such towering figures as Marcel Mauss, Victor Turner and Clifford Geertz, to mention only three (for a good sampling of the history of anthropological views of ritual, for example, see Bell 1992). The reader has to make the connections: the lectures that were left behind simply do not. There is also little or no sustained attention to alternative accounts of the examples he offers or to the general historical context of Tanna (Vanuatu) at the time he was writing. Of course, the interested reader can consult other authorities and *The Tree and the Canoe* to place what Bonnemaison has to say here in this wider frame of reference. For example, the writings of anthropologists such as Lamont Lindstrom

(1993) and Jean Guiart (e.g. 1996), although the latter author seems to feel diminished by the high regard in which Bonnemaison's work has been held, offer somewhat different readings of eastern Melanesia in the 1980s and 1990s. This book also proffers little or no guidance as to Bonnemaison's overall conception of European colonialism and how it might continue to affect the interpretations of scholars of European origin such as himself. For many years a researcher with the French government development-research organization, ORSTOM (now IRD), Bonnemaison was obviously mindful of the post-colonial context in which he worked. In *The Tree and the Canoe* he certainly showed considerable concern for his social 'positionality' relative to that of the people who served as his informants. He was painfully aware of the difficulties of the non-indigenous researcher attempting to represent a culture so different from his own. But this theme is not strongly evident in the lectures. It is currently, however, a major and persisting preoccupation of some anglophone cultural geographers (see, e.g. Clayton 2003). Last of all, the book misses one of the main features of Bonnemaison, the person and author, which is of someone who had a poetic way with words. This does show through in the translation of his magnum opus *The Tree and the Canoe* but it is largely missing here because of the degree of reconstruction that necessarily had to go into putting the fragments together.

Every book is always and inevitably a work in progress. All writers hope that they can revisit what they have written previously to elaborate on what they wrote and to address questions left unasked. Sadly, in this case this is not possible. It is the fact that there is any book at all that needs to be accented. The book is above all a testament to the devotion that Joël Bonnemaison inspired in so many people around the world (see, e.g. Guillaud et al. 1998; Waddell 1999). Perhaps it was his evident sense of wonder about the rich variety of humanity that rubbed off on others. Perhaps it was his own deep humanity that left a lasting impression. One thing is for sure: not only his students in Paris, but his neighbours in Gascony, his colleagues in France, Australia and elsewhere, and his friends and informants in Vanuatu all wish he was still around to do the job for them. But because he is not, they have done it in memory of him. From these pages you can get some idea of what it was that inspired them to do so. The hope must be that his cultural geography will live on after him as more people become familiar with it. Publication of this volume in English is one small step in that direction.

Acknowledgement

I would like to acknowledge the assistance of Josée Pénot-Demetry (The Ecospace Institute), David Stonestreet (I.B. Tauris), Denis Cosgrove (UCLA), Felicity Nussbaum (UCLA), Lamont Lindstrom (University of Tulsa) and Joel Robbins (UC, San Diego) in bringing the translation to fruition and in giving advice on this Introduction to the English edition.

1

Introduction

Cultural geography positions human beings at the centre of geographical knowledge – human beings, with their beliefs, their passions, and their life experiences.[1] Cultural geography is meant to be a human science, a specific approach to the lives of people. It investigates the relevance of culture throughout today's world; it deals with symbols as much as with facts, and emotions as much as reason.

> ### From the nature of space to the space of culture
>
> *Social and cultural images of an island space*
>
> My initial question deals with the concept of 'space': is there an original relation between nature and culture? More exactly, is there an analogy between *mental* organization and *natural* organization of space? Does such a fertile analogy have an effect on cultural organization, social images, founding myths, organizing metaphors and symbols, all of which give meaning to social creation and give shape to landscape – the latter being both the 'imprint' and the 'matrix' of this worldview?
>
> In other words, is there fertile cross-breeding between nature and culture? Is there a type of osmosis between the nature of a world and the spirit of a civilization, a sort of

transformation that spatial organization and the shaping of landscape translate visually and therefore geographically?

Here I am not inverting the widely accepted trope that 'space is produced by society', because I would then fall into an idealistic view that a geographer would find difficult to accept. Instead, I wish to balance out the space/society relationship by adding a cultural dimension that is often lacking. Space may be produced by society, yet society creates itself within a cultural space. I think there are several levels of understanding: if cultural geography exists (i.e. if it is more than an intellectual game), it exists because, beyond the system of production and beyond history, there is an *initial place*[2] – or, to put it differently, a perception tied to a mental organization – that is born from the creative osmosis between a specific natural environment and the small number of great founding myths that explain it. This 'preliminary place' must be defined for each society. From it, space is shaped and, through it, a web of values and meanings is organized. This perspective gives an understanding of Melanesian societies in Oceania, for example. At the beginning of all things is the island world – a *natural environment*. Then a canoe appears, thanks to which one can journey to an island – *the physical environment of a society* that originally is itself a 'wandering island' and a group of navigators. These 'epic beginnings' give rise to a perception, a symbolism and a series of social and cultural images that make up a culture or, alternatively, 'a vision of the world'. Such a vision is not expressed by means of a constructed discourse or ideology but through images and metaphors that give rise to thoughts and representations. Within this vision, space is perceived as a cluster of islands linked by roads, and society is a canoe that follows these roads. Hence space does not abide by the hallowed core–periphery model: spatial organization is network-like – a 'fabric of nexus' and a fluid web. Space is not a centre with

> margins; rather it is a road with a beginning and an infinite end, farther on. The landscape reproduces this image and society arranges itself upon it.
>
> J. Bonnemaison, 'De la nature de l'espace à l'espace de la culture: images sociales et culturelles d'un espace insulaire', *L'Espace géographique*, 1 (1985), 33.

My interest for cultural geography did not evolve by chance but is rooted in the research topics I have investigated in the course of a long career, first in Madagascar (1965), then eastward to Vanuatu in 1968, and finally Australia in 1985.

I first examined rural society, agricultural transformation and economic development. I then did research on migration networks and the urbanization of migrants. As I became increasingly interested in the cultural aspects of development, I started looking into ethnogeography and cultural geography.

Rural studies (*Étude de terroirs*) and the evolution of agricultural systems

Madagascar (1965–67)

My first field study was along the lines of rural studies[3] as they were then carried out at ORSTOM (now IRD)[4] under the enlightened guidance of Gilles Sautter and Paul Pélissier.

The place I surveyed was a village called Tsarahonenana, in Madagascar's Ankaratra mountainous region. My goal was to analyse how the agricultural system was adapted to the environment and how the village could adjust to the constraints of the market economy. In brief, I had to assess the development potential of a traditional agricultural system.

In Ankaratra, rice paddies are situated at elevations of 1,700 to 1,800 metres and farmers irrigate rice in valley lowlands up to 2,000 metres. Yet agricultural experts categorically assert that cultivating irrigated rice above 1,500 metres is not 'profitable'. The irrigation water is too cold, the growing season too short, and as a consequence the yields are small and uncertain.

The Ankaratra farmers are settlers of Merina origin, who relocated there one or two centuries ago. They were rice growers *par excellence* in their place of origin and continue to be so in their adopted land. Not only do the Merina grow and eat rice but they are expected to devote paddy surpluses to exchange competitions in honour of their ancestors. The awareness of their ethnic identity cannot be separated from their rice-growing practices. Therefore the Merina keep on being rice growers – despite a mountain environment that is not well suited for this type of cultivation.

These settler-farmers are also involved in a secondary commercial crop – potatoes – that is well adapted to their new natural environment: they go to a neighbouring village to sell their crop, using the proceeds to buy the extra rice they need for food and for ancestor-honouring rituals. The monetary surplus from this secondary culture offsets the structural weakness of rice cultivation. Merina farmers are both determined rice growers and tireless potato producers and shipment experts.

But it is not so much the search for productivity, profitability, or even a new speculative crop that animates the farmers of Tsarahonenana. What is most important is that they are determined to replicate the agricultural system of their cultural origins in a high-elevation environment, even though that environment is ill suited for the task. Merina society lives within its own cultural universe; once survival is assured, ancestors are as important as the living. Merina settlers of the Ankaratra 'produce' within a pre-capitalistic framework: values that are essentially religious shape their cultural vision. By acting in that manner, they continue to be 'human beings'[5] according to Merina civilization. They plant rice despite the advice of agronomists.

Agricultural systems and societies in Vanuatu

After being posted in Oceania I carried out several long-term research projects in Vanuatu (then called the New Hebrides). These allowed me to deepen my understanding of the cultural aspects of rural societies and their development.

In the course of this research I progressively evolved from the classical socio-economic approach on agrarian structures to a wider, territory-based, socio-cultural angle. What led me to this new approach was my research on land tenure systems and the utilization of island environments.

Pacific island systems are very diverse. For instance, seashore communities cultivate yams whereas mountain communities grow taro. Such a distinction is not related to ecological constraints but seems to be a cultural trait, in so far as it calls for exchange and thereby facilitates 'blood alliances' between local groups that are either allies or enemies. Each group is specialized – producing what another does not possess, or possesses in small quantities. Local groups carefully attend to their differences so that they can better exchange their products. They follow a cultural or political logic more than an economic one, thereby avoiding a mimicry that could be dangerous in an island context. In turn, their specialized, complementary economic and ritual activities make alliances mandatory.

The Melanesian agricultural system is built on a paradox. Practices such as the use of shifting gardens, various forms of clearing and planting, the lack of permanent land parcels, and gathering activities, which are still widespread, are all part of the general system of extensive slash-and-burn agriculture. Within this Indonesian *ladang* type of agriculture, Melanesians create islands of intensive cultivation. They use irrigation and drainage techniques in taro

fields or grow yam tubers on large mounds, which make up localized areas of intensive cultivation in the midst of a production
system that is globally extensive. Plentiful taro and large yams
from such enclaves are mostly intended for exchange in the course
of rituals of alliance. The type and magnitude of these rituals vary
among islands and cultural areas.

In other words, Melanesians from traditional societies had knowledge of agrarian techniques that would have allowed them to
intensify their production system, yet they did not think it necessary to develop them. They apparently refused to jump into an
intensive mode of production that would have shattered their
social and spatial organization. From the outset, political (or cultural) factors were considered more important than economic
motives. Intensive production, thus confined to the realm of the
'beautiful', represents ritual production for exchange and alliance
purposes while extensive production facilitates day-to-day
subsistence.

Migration networks and the urbanization of migrants

In the early 1970s, the Anglo-French government of the New
Hebrides Condominium asked me to study migratory flows
involving the archipelago's two urban areas. Through different
paths this new type of research eventually led to the same issues.

My survey of migration patterns outlined two types of network.
The first network dealt with a series of temporary migrations over
relatively short distances and of short duration, in other words, a
process called *circulation*. In contrast, the second network entailed
a long-term or even permanent form of migration – a kind of rural
outmigration.

Traditional communities control circulation: structured groups,
tied to their community of origin, establish themselves in urban

areas and strive to control certain sectors of the labour market. Migrants stay within the circle of their fellow islanders and move back to their home village periodically. This type of migration is neither an 'uprooting' nor a 'rural outmigration' but a form of circular mobility that is in line with traditional Melanesian journeying and remains under the control of traditional leaders.

The second migration pattern can be called 'wild' in so far as it is uncontrolled and unforeseen. It takes place within the margins of circular mobility and has a more individualistic connotation: links with the community of origin become blurred and return trips are less frequent.

As a rule, circular mobility is community-based and occurs within the most 'customary' societies: the depth of traditional culture explains the strong linkages with the territories of origin and the cohesiveness of group structures. In contrast, wild mobility reveals features that developed in coastal societies as these became acculturated and locked into the trade-based plantation economy. Along with schooling and disregard for 'custom' came the progressive loss of territorial ties, the weakening of group links and, as a counterpart, the emergence of a desire for 'urban mobility' that needs to find personal expression.

All my research topics kept bringing me back to the values of 'custom' as they are confronted with the modern world. On that account I decided to investigate the cultural geography of the communities considered to be the most traditional. My doctoral thesis, *Les Fondements d'une identité: territoire, histoire et société, dans l'archipel de Vanuatu (Mélanésie)* (Foundations of an identity: territory, history and society in the archipelago of Vanuatu (Melanesia))[6], summarized the attempt.

Melanesian territory and cultural dimensions

My new research pursued four major themes: the spatial organization of traditional societies, its linkages with founding myths, the
connections between social system and spatial system, and the
structuring effect of territory on society. Perhaps the most
important idea that came out of that research is that Melanesian
island society follows a network model within a space that is not
'core and periphery'-based but reticulated. Two factors may
explain such a model: the political will to create an egalitarian society and the determination to transcend the constraints of
geographic insularity.

In a world of islands where nature only offers discontinuous spaces
and threatened morsels of land, Melanesian society endeavoured to
recreate continuity by building a fluid social space, a web of multiple relationships. Within each place in the network, it then
invented an enchanted space, full of magic and secrets, and built a
space of plenitude by fully diversifying its territory.

Melanesian space is the result of this process. It is a complex network, a flexible and reticulated system of places and roads of
alliance, weaving nexus upon nexus around various places of
confluence, which themselves are connected with spatial configurations farther away. Melanesian places and groups exist as links
within a chain of relations that extends from island to island and
from one archipelago to the next. Rather than an enclosed space,
Oceanian territory is a road of alliance connecting local groups that
are sovereign and distinct, and even in some cases very far from
each other.

Reticulated space takes shape as a network where each place and
therefore each group is the equal complement to the place or group
before and after it on the road. Society can only operate through
the consensus of each of the sovereign links that are part of the
same road of alliance. In political terms, the territory is not a *pré
carré*,[7] a classic system organized by a state and marked out by

frontiers, but an interdependent link within a system of relations that spreads well beyond its own limits and delineates wide spatial configurations of alliance.

Within reticulated space, the focal place is not a central place but a founding place. The territory is not organized according to the centralized-polygon or core-and-periphery models but according to a nexus-shaped model. The founding place brings forth a road-like space where messages, political relations and rituals of alliance jump along from one link to the next. There is no allegiance in such a system but only precedence. Accordingly, Melanesian leadership is based on honour rather than power. Efficient mediators called 'Big Men' hold predominant political roles, organizing exchanges and weaving social links.

In 1985 I defended my doctoral thesis, *Les Fondements d'une identité: territoire, histoire et société, dans l'archipel de Vanuatu (Mélanésie)*. This was followed by the publication of *La Dernière île*[8] and its English translation, *The Tree and the Canoe: History and Ethnogeography of Tanna*.[9] These works were both the outcome of my research and the starting point for a new approach based on reticulated space and cultural geography.

Reticulated space

Today, the scope of my research has become wider, both in regional and thematic terms, as I continue to investigate two major issues:

- Development and dependence within the context of Oceania, a region characterized by insularity, multiple archipelagic states and feuds over the issue of identity.
- Representations and concepts regarding (a) networks and (b) the shaping of reticulated space, seemingly the most innovative themes.

I was posted at the Australian National University (ANU) in Canberra for two years, which allowed me to work at the macrogeographic scale of the South Pacific as a whole.

Melanesian societies are 'stateless societies'. Political power is gained through prestige competitions and relations of exchange. Society is an open arena where the glory of great men and the power of 'Big Men' are set in motion. In order to be effective, power implies the consensus of subordinates; it also entails numerous polemics and political compromises. Power rarely extends beyond the geographic scale of a local group, which generally amounts to a few hundred people. This segmented society coincides with a splintered political space made up of multiple and competing places. Therefore space is not unified by a core that 'produces' a periphery that it dominates. Rather, networks of equal groups delineate space; these groups are allies or enemies, often alternately one and then the other. Political space has no actual centre or periphery but manifests itself as a broken line with numerous political nodes extending into secondary autonomous networks. The latter spread over neighbouring space, as befits the geographical nature of island environments.

Over these flexible structures contemporary politics superimposes the rigid organizing principle of the nation-state copied from the Western world. As a consequence, ancient network relations are severed or must be redefined: a core node appears, around which a periphery is born. Space becomes unbending, yesterday's flexibility fades away and the state apparatus girdles society. This takeover by the nation-state causes tensions; new problems appear. Centrifugal forces and libertarian movements, more or less organized, attempt to unsettle the new structure; they try to boost the autonomy of local groups, which the nation's unfaltering goal is to eradicate, be it consciously or not.

A state apparatus is costly and obviously beyond the limited means of South Pacific micro-nations. Public administration operates thanks to external aid supplied by the larger nations. Foreign aid often takes the form of direct budgetary funds transferred directly from country to country. In return, the archipelagic nations of Oceania enter a spiralling dependence. They reach the last stage of this process when national dependence on foreign aid is accompanied by the dependence of their citizens on remittances from migrants who have gone out to Sydney, Honolulu, Auckland, or Nouméa to work. As it becomes dependent on the nation-state and outmigration, local society is hemmed in by an artificial structure that perpetuates a false situation. A number of small island-nations have reached this stage. In other words, *small is not* (always) *beautiful*,[10] since smallness in this case implies extreme fragility and creates dangerous dependences.

In 1988 I edited the *Atlas des îles et États du Pacifique sud* (Atlas of islands and states of the South Pacific) in joint collaboration with Benoît Antheaume.[11]

Benoît Antheaume and I also jointly edited the Oceania portion of the seventh volume (entitled *Asie du Sud-Est, Océanie* – Southeast Asia and Oceania) in the *Géographie universelle*, Elisée Reclus commemorative edition, under the general direction of Roger Brunet.[12] I surveyed the 'wide spaces' of Australia, a type of terrain that is quite different from the geography of small island-nations. I applied the cultural approach I had used in Melanesia to a much larger scale, that of a continent with a modern Western society, and tested the validity of that approach. I used the same themes: networks, territories as archipelagos connected together by many different types of flows, places and territories of identity, and the dialectics of mobility and stability.

Seeing places as unique 'geographical beings' is what interests me, yet I always try to coordinate that aspect with a more general research focus on the cultural dimension of regions and territories. The latter, I believe, is absolutely essential to studying social development.

Cultural geography research

Since 1994, I have been teaching undergraduate and graduate cultural geography at the University of Paris IV Sorbonne. This is a novel field with no acknowledged theory or even a well-circumscribed scope. It has now become of interest to many researchers, allowing for numerous innovations and intellectual advances as far as societies and their relation to space are concerned. I now wish to devote my research to this topic primarily. My goal is to explore the new avenues of cultural geography and to deepen its links with other social sciences, notably anthropology.

In the short term I wish to teach, oversee student research and reflect on the cultural foundations of human geography: in brief, address the issues dealing with the geography of cultures and the anthropology of space. Through my teaching and perhaps through a book I may write later, I hope to enhance my extensive experience as an ORSTOM/IRD researcher in the field of development studies, in liaison with researchers from other disciplines.

Development studies carried out by ORSTOM/IRD researchers touch upon culture when they search to explain the variation in development levels between societies and, generally speaking, whenever they account for spatial discontinuities. Therefore development studies can contribute very effectively to research on cultural geography, both in terms of meaning and of content.

I believe that researchers need to alternate professional experiences with participation in the management of research, carving time for reflection and carrying out knowledge transfer. When we teach at a university, be it temporarily or permanently, we organize that knowledge, put it to the test in front of an audience, contribute to the training of young researchers, and try to reach a synthesis that compartmentalized research processes may not have allowed us to attain earlier in our careers. Is there anything more interesting for us than to be able to expand our field while giving larger meaning to our original approach?

2

The revival of the cultural approach

Cultural geography is a novel idea. More precisely, geographers still argue about it today. The term may be puzzling to some, as if culture – a discipline of the mind – and geography – a concrete, material, naturalistic discipline, tied to facts and space – had little to do together. Within the traditional framework of the social sciences, culture seems to 'belong' to ethnologists, anthropologists and sociologists, whereas nature and environment are the province of geographers.

Why a *cultural* geography, then, and what purpose does it serve?

At the outset, I must say that geographers have, on occasion, questioned the value of that approach. Although the term itself is new, the concept of cultural geography is not. It first appeared in Germany, German geographers being less 'naturalistic' than French geographers: in the nineteenth century, Friedrich Ratzel already spoke of anthropo-geography. Cultural geography returned to France via the United States where it had attained a measure of success – thanks to the works of Carl Sauer, a disciple of Ratzel and founder of the Berkeley school. In France the process was actually more a revival than a birth. With their renewed emphasis on culture, French-speaking geographers from Quebec greatly influenced that renaissance in the 1980s. The revival did go with the grain of the French school of geography – for there is such a thing as a specifically French approach to cultural geography. Several factors may explain this recent re-discovery.

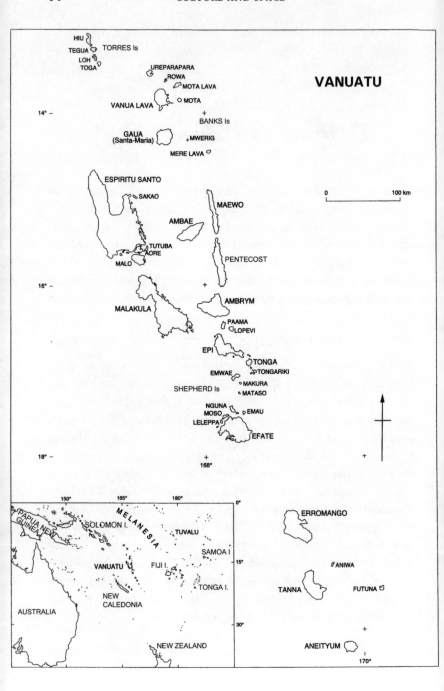

HIU
TEGUA   TORRES Is
LOH
TOGA

UREPARAPARA
ROWA
MOTA LAVA
VANUA LAVA   MOTA

14° –   +
BANKS Is

GAUA   MWERIG
(Santa-Maria)
MERE LAVA

VANUATU

0   100 km

ESPIRITU SANTO

SAKAO   MAEWO

AMBAE
TUTUBA
AORE
MALO   PENTECOST

16° –   +

MALAKULA   AMBRYM

PAAMA
LOPEVI

EPI
TONGA
EMWAE   TONGARIKI
MAKURA
SHEPHERD Is   MATASO

NGUNA   EMAU
MOSO
LELEPPA
EFATE

18° –   +
168°

MELANESIA

150°   165°   180°

PAPUA NEW
GUINEA
SOLOMON I.   TUVALU   0°

SAMOA I

VANUATU   FIJI I.   15°

NEW
CALEDONIA   TONGA I.

AUSTRALIA

30°

NEW ZEALAND

ERROMANGO

ANIWA

TANNA   FUTUNA

ANEITYUM
170°

First, the renaissance of cultural geography is linked to the expansion of the term 'culture'. People of my generation used to say: 'everything is political'. Today, 'everything is cultural'. Hence there is *a fashion about culture*. We now talk about company culture, the culture of political parties, and so forth; each activity, each human group possesses its own culture. There is even a Ministry of Culture within the French government. Culture has invaded other social sciences besides geography. As a matter of fact, social scientists often define as 'cultural' any factor that is qualitative and non-quantifiable, although this type of negative definition hardly allows for a thorough analysis of issues.

The success of the cultural approach in geography rests also – and perhaps primarily – on a certain disillusion regarding 'radical geography' and 'the new geography'.

André Malraux[1] defined the twentieth century as *'the century of ideology'*. Today we put less faith in the grand ideologies that led to two world wars. Marxism, in particular, claims to explain everything on the basis of class relations and production structures; this elementary vision does not take culture into account. Marxism has had a strong influence on the 'radical geography' practised in anglophone countries. Geoculture, considered as a 'superstructure', does not appear in neo-Marxist writings. Antonio Gramsci, however, thought that Italians practised an *'erroneous reading of culture'*, which he defined as a power that could subvert political and economic forces.[2]

The rebirth of cultural geography is also tied to the evolution of some positivistic social sciences, such as sociology, economics and the 'new geography'. All at one point have pronounced themselves exact sciences, similar to physics or mathematics, the so-called 'hard sciences'. According to that trend, scientific laws explain the organization of human beings and space through economic, social and, of course, spatial structures. Thus, the spatial distribution of human populations and activities follows laws that can be discovered through the use of quasi-mathematical models (Harvey

1989). The issue is still being debated today. Generally speaking, the quantitative approach, although fruitful, is much less 'totalitarian' than twenty years ago, when there was 'no salvation outside of the quantitative'. The 'new geography', as it was called in the 1960s, is less ambitious today. It gives more room to the cultural approach, which does not necessarily contradict it and, in truth, makes it whole.

Radical, Marxist geography and the 'new' positivistic geography reigned from the 1960s to the 1980s. They slandered each other although they had the same 'materialist' or 'hard science' approach. During the reign of the new geography, several current proponents of cultural geography were on field study in exotic locales.[3]

The revival of cultural geography benefited from the outstanding works of individuals who dared to call themselves 'cultural geographers'. First among them is Paul Claval, who made this branch of geography relevant again, notably by analysing its genesis and development (1995a, 1995b). The school of tropical geography, with pioneers such as Pierre Gourou, Jean Gallais and Gilles Sautter, also played an important role. All these researchers surveyed distinctive cultures, ethnic groups and civilizations with a particular emphasis on their unique or specific features. Augustin Berque has done research about landscape (both 'imprint and matrix of culture') and Japanese culture, which does not dissociate physical features from human characteristics in a given milieu – also known as *fudo*. Finally the list should include the names of Jean-Robert Pitte, Xavier de Planhol and Pierre Flatrès at the University of Paris IV.

My own research is immersed in a cultural universe that is radically different: that of cargo cults, myths and representations. In *La Dernière île* (translated as *The Tree and the Canoe*) I write about the revolt that the people of Tanna carried out in the name of custom. I reflect about the links between the islanders' cultural identity, proclaimed as such, and geographical space, or rather the islanders' representation of space: a landscape that is both 'seen' (or acknowledged)[4] and 'enchanted' (or made sacred).

The three dimensions of landscape-space within cultural geography are as follows:

- *A territory* that involves geopolitical stakes and a boundary; a political structure with centres, cores and margins.
- *A geographical setting*: an ecological and geographical structure – soils, vegetation, hydrology, climate, human density, communication network. Human beings fully belong to this ecological system because all geographical environments are anthropomorphized to a smaller or greater extent.
- *A geosymbolism*: the symbolic structure of a geographical setting; its signification. The notion is similar to that of '*médiance*' as presented by Augustin Berque (1990).[5] Human beings inscribe and illustrate their values in landscape. Geosymbols, which give meaning to the world, are related to ethics and metaphysics. They represent the spirituality of a place – what we call the spirit of a place.

The renewed importance of the cultural approach in geography is nothing more than the application to our discipline of the more general renewal of the cultural dimension, notably in linguistics, anthropology (called cultural anthropology to differentiate it from social anthropology) and economics (witness the popularity of economic anthropology, as opposed to econometrics). Great thinkers in those disciplines have analysed cultural systems or structures and suggested new paradigms. Among these thinkers are Claude Lévi-Strauss and linguist and anthropologist Georges Dumézil, two internationally known figures of French anthropology.

Dumézil's work primarily deals with Indo-European language and mythology. Dumézil demonstrates that the original Indo-European language had induced a number of myths. These myths in turn facilitate the investigation of social and ideological models. Thus, Dumézil outlines three basic social functions – political, religious and economic – that used to exist in various societies from

India to Ireland, such as French society before the Revolution at the end of the eighteenth century. It is worth noting that Dumézil's structuralism is much less rigid than Lévi-Strauss's.

Economics and the fulfilment of material interests are reducing factors that can only cast a limited light on human beings. A more complete explanation includes a person's value system as well as his/her mind and emotions, wish for territory and search for ideals and the absolute. In brief, a human being may be defined as a complex cultural and affective construction. 'Man does not live by bread alone.' Where does he find his sustenance? This 'supplement of soul' involves culture …

The cultural approach within geography is the subject matter of this course, which will, by necessity, be incomplete since much still remains to be investigated. That mystery is, in part, what makes cultural geography so fascinating.

The three bases of
contemporary human geography

The German school of cultural geography
(Landschaft geography and political geography)

Concurrently with the birth of the German nation-state, the German school emerges in the nineteenth century under the impetus of Kant's Geography. To German geographers, the idea of nation is intertwined with that of culture, both soul and expression of an entire people. Culture feeds the dream of national unity and the search for identity. These geographers are philosophers and naturalists that abide by the universal message of the Enlightenment. They are eager to understand the fate of peoples and nations: hence, their main topic of interest is the relation of collective beings with their natural environment, with landscape. German geographers reflect on the following issues: what is the meaning of differences on the surface of the earth? Are cultural differences inherent to environmental differences? Does the diverging fate of nations depend on such differences? Is there a determinism that explains the common fate of peoples?

Spatial differentiation as a geographical topic

At the outset, geography is seen as a science of the joint history of nature and humanity. As the philosophical originator of the modern concept of 'nation', Gottfried Herder (1744–1803) binds geography to the historical approach. Herder emphasizes the role played by cultural communities in the construction of landscapes and spaces. According to Herder, the aim of geography is to recreate the spatial and natural framework of a people's history. Herder delineates homogeneous spaces and territories within which various forms of ethnicity and culture are established; hence the *spatial differentiation* of the world. The uniqueness[6] of a people does not originate in a vacuum: it is born from its fusion with an earth that it fits out and scatters with geosymbols. A people expresses its uniqueness by using the environment optimally, by creating a landscape specific to its culture and, in an inverse dialectical process, by letting that space influence its culture. A people's political destiny is thus inscribed in its historical and natural space. According to Herder, to develop the concept of a modern nation – in the sense of a geographical being endowed with a mind (culture) and a body (earth) – is equivalent to reaching a new stage toward universal progress.

The naturalist philosopher Carl Ritter (1779–1859) extends Herder's intuitions to his own analysis of human–environment relations. Ritter emphasizes the determining influence of the natural environment upon the origin and evolution of civilizations. He also articulates the essential dialectics of spatial scales by envisioning the municipality, then the region, the country, the nation, the cultural area and, finally the world, as *nested* spaces.

The humanistic spirit of Alexander von Humboldt (1769–1859) gives a boost to the German school of geography. A traveller, naturalist and scientist, Humboldt uses his powerful and passionate mind to synthesize knowledge by linking and comparing cultures and environments. One of his French disciples, Elisée Reclus (1830–1905), is the author of the encyclopedic *Nouvelle géographie universelle*, written between 1876 and 1894.

When, in 1883, Friedrich Ratzel (1844–1904), publishes his *Anthropogeography*, this zoologist by training makes a crucial contribution to the rich lineage of German geography. Ratzel integrates the ideas of culture and nature, which, combined with social Darwinism, make up the ideological framework of his time. Ratzel is able to complete the analysis of vertical relations between a society and its environment with a horizontal relation; he expounds the concept of *diffusionism* or propagation of cultural traits from an original hearth. Ratzel wonders about the influence of the environment on the evolution of humankind as he deals with the issue of *geographic determinism*, to which he prefers the term *possibilism*, with its vast array of nuances. With Ratzel, geography wavers: that uncertainty is still with us today. Peoples and cultures are steeped in the environment where they are born, where they evolve, which they transform, and which they explain to themselves. Some peoples or cultures are the product of this adaptive process while others liberate themselves from the environment. Ratzel raises one major philosophical issue about giving their respective due to nature (and all that is determined by nature) on the one hand and culture, history and economics on the other.

Founding concepts of German geography: environment, landscape and nation

Focusing on the diversity of peoples and landscapes, and patterning itself on the natural sciences, German geography elaborates doctrines and methods that give it the status of a science, albeit not a social but a natural science of society. Geography uses logical empiricism to deal with one major issue, that of *spatial differentiation*. Under the enlightened joint influence of naturalism and Darwinism, societies are perceived as quasi-biological organisms that compete with each other. German geopolitics derives from this line of thought. Ratzel, the founder of geopolitics, sees space as a place of power, a material incarnation of the State, and the true corporeal soul of the people.

The descriptive approach of German geography is based on several concepts. Physical geography is first naturalistic, then evolves into an environmental science that gives rise to the idea of *geographic setting* and humankind's relation to it. Humboldt originates this key concept. He shows that asymmetries in climate among continental shores are due to oceanic currents, such as the one that bears his name. Humboldt describes similar climates – cold, temperate and hot – and introduces the concept of *natural milieu*.

Using the idea of *landscape* as an expression of culture, geography becomes the science of landscape (*Landschaftskunde*).[7] That approach allows us to understand, and even compare, the ability of peoples and nations to establish a harmonious relation with nature and to construct that relation as a landscape. The definition of the word *Landschaft* itself refers to the symbiosis between landscape, image and country. According to Ratzel, culture merges with environment. In Germany, this idea will eventually give rise to a romanticized view of landscape, tinged with nationalism.

At the same time, Ratzel develops the concept of *nation* as a major geographical actor. Collective beings are perceived as political beings with their own memories, dreams and rivalries. Ratzel emphasizes the role of the State in the destiny and evolution of peoples. In Ratzel's eyes, Germany is the Middle Empire – *Mittel-Europa* – in the image of China, which itself structures Asia. The great contribution of Ratzel was to analyse and structure the world into large continental masses solidified around core spaces. According to Ratzel, the destiny of peoples is subservient to their geographical destiny. Along those lines, the destiny of the German nation is to assume a role of central power at the heart of Europe. German geostrategy will later derive from geopolitics; Karl Haushofer, a disciple of Ratzel, developed this theme during the most tragic phase of the twentieth century.[8]

Today the concepts of landscape, milieu and culture are at the heart of the cultural approach in geography. The cultural approach reinstated each human being as both a social individual and a unique being. It also revitalized human geography. At the same time, and more empirically, it aimed at differentiating itself from political geography.

The French school of geography

The French school is based on the German tradition. Its founding father is Paul Vidal de la Blache (1845–1918), who launched the concept of *geographic region*.

The founding father: Paul Vidal de la Blache

In his capacity as a teacher at École Normale Supérieure,[9] Vidal de la Blache converted a number of young historians to geography: in particular, Jean Brunhes, Emmanuel de Martonne, Albert Demangeon and Jules Sion, the actual founders of the French school. Vidal de la Blache elevated the discipline. He tackled two major issues: (1) the mapping of demographic differences and (2) the regional diversity of terrestrial space.

The regional school

Vidal de la Blache begins with the traditional French model: the national territory with its ancient localities, or '*pays*', and its regions. Localities are *geographic beings* that derive from a combination of physical laws, bio-geological laws and human realities. Regions are steeped in a historical reality made up of actual structures that transcend and even survive political divisions: simply put, what anchors regions is permanence rather than change. As for the nation, it is a harmonious totality that integrates various regional components. The diversity of terrestrial space illustrates the juxtaposition of regional structures, which is what geography investigates.

For Vidal de la Blache, 'geography is not the science of humankind but that of places'. Geography considers human beings only in so far as they shape and manage landscape. This type of geography is resolutely *possibilistic* rather than deterministic: nature makes suggestions, human beings pick and choose.

Genre de vie

Each region is based on a natural environment to which humans adapt themselves by using a natural element as intermediary, either a plant or an animal, such as rice in Asia or pigs in Melanesia (for instance, pigs with curved tusks in Vanuatu). This selection process gives rise to a *genre de vie* or lifeway.[10] A *genre de vie* is what a group selects from a variety of natural elements in order to create a favourable life environment and build its culture. In essence, human geography investigates the vital activities that govern lifeways.

Pigs with curved tusks in Vanuatu

The 'hierarchy of grades', as ethnologists call it, is widespread throughout [the northern part of the Vanuatu archipelago] [...]. A man attains a grade by means of a test that has an economic foundation; the effort is all the more complex and exacting as the grade level is high. The postulant must pay for all rituals linked with a specific grade and must sacrifice pigs whose value is commensurate with the rank attained. [...] Pigs are bred for this purpose: once its upper canines are removed, the animal's lower canines grow into curved tusks, which may reach a complete circle or even a circle and a half. To each growth stage correspond a name and a particular value [...]. A man pays for his grade by slaughtering pigs that are also graded, i.e. that are more or less valuable [...].

In the north of the archipelago, breeders endeavour not so much to produce a large number of pigs as to raise pigs with curved tusks for ceremonial purposes [...]. Within traditional society, men spend more time obtaining this type of goods than gathering the products that allow them to survive *stricto sensu*.

Tusked-pig breeding is a time-consuming and difficult undertaking that entails a large number of losses. The process begins with neutered males, about two years old. The breeder pulls out the upper canines against which the lower tusks are abutting. The two tusks then slowly grow in the shape of a circle. As they curve around, the tusks grow in the direction of the upper sides of the animal's face, which they pierce, then spiral downward. This is a decisive stage: the tusks, after going through their first circle, are likely to hit the lower jaw, pushing into and pulling out the other teeth, and ultimately causing the animal to die. If everything goes well, however, the tusks will glide over the jaw and begin a second internal circle that parallels the first circle. The pig is now acknowledged as a great pig. It is given a name and the success of the endeavour becomes known throughout the region. Its breeder prides himself on this favourable outcome, which he has brought about by means of his techniques and magical practices.

In this search for the impossible, the utmost achievement was the growth, complete or incomplete, of a third circle within the first two spirals. Such an animal was at least thirty years old, a canonical age, and was venerated as a live ancestor [...]. A two-and-a-half-circled tusk was offered to the Queen of England when she last visited the Anglo-French condominium of the New Hebrides before independence.

Obviously this practice is an excruciating torture for the animal, because it can no longer feed itself. Women have to mash food and sometimes chew it themselves before slipping it into the pig's mouth so that the animal may swallow it [...]. Today, ceremonial pigs are raised in small stone or wood enclosures. In the past, they lived alongside the islanders. The most precious pigs even slept in the *nakamal* or men's house, sharing foods and domestic space.

J. Bonnemaison, *Gens de pirogue et gens de la terre. Les fondements géographiques d'une identité: l'archipel du Vanuatu* (revised edition of *L'Arbre et la pirogue*), Paris, ORSTOM, 1996, 123–6, 258–61.

Paul Vidal de la Blache's disciples

Vidal de la Blache had many followers. Emmanuel de Martonne (1873–1955) developed physical geography as one of the early pioneers of geomorphology, which under his guidance became the most prestigious field within the discipline. Jean Brunhes (1869–1940) was the founder of human geography, which he saw as the investigation of humanity's imprint on earth. Brunhes's own talented disciple, Pierre Deffontaines (1894–1978) created a series of 'human geography' publications often entitled *L'Homme et ...* (Man and ...).[11] Lucien Gallois, Albert Demangeon, Jules Sion, Max Sorre and Henri Baulig were the authors of *Géographie universelle* in twenty volumes (1927–48, under the initial direction of Vidal de la Blache).

Criticism of Paul Vidal de la Blache

The first criticism came from geopolitics. According to Yves Lacoste, the Vidalian region-place not only hides social reality but also creates a misconception regarding the determining role of politics. Additionally, Vidal minimizes the role of towns since regions, as he defines them, are primarily rural. The sharpest critics were

A ceremonial pig tusk and its successive grades
(N. E. Ambae)

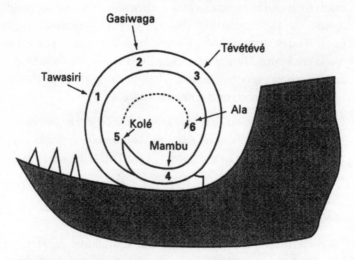

1 Tawasiri: pig tusks begin to grow in a curve
2 Gasiwaga: the tusks begin to pierce the jowls
3 Tévétévé: while inside the mouth, the tusks grow closer to the lower jaw
4 Mambu: the tusks glide over the lower jaw
5 Kolé: the tusks start to form a second spiral inside the first circle
6 Ala: the tusks complete, or are in the process of completing, their second spiral

After the upper canines are removed, pig tusks grow into a spiral. According to custom, each stage of their growth corresponds to a 'grade' and to a specific value. Once their first run is completed, the tusks begin a second run. Pigs are like life: 'When it is over, it starts once again'.

J. Bonnemaison, *Gens de pirogue et gens de la terre. Les fondements géographiques d'une identité: l'archipel du Vanuatu* (revised edition of *L'Arbre et la pirogue*), Paris, ORSTOM, 1996, 259.

Marxist geographers, whom the concept of region prevented from looking at space as a product of social and economic factors. Finally, other disciplines rebelled against the idea of geography as a 'synthesizing science'. They only wanted to see it as a branch of the natural sciences with no relevance in the social arena.

Response to criticism

Yves Lacoste has changed his mind since these early criticisms. In an article in the journal *Hérodote,* 'A bas Vidal, viva Vidal' ('Down with Vidal, long live Vidal'), Lacoste says that Vidal de la Blache was the first among French geographers to pay attention to politics – a precursor to geopolitics, so to speak, in particular as far as the urban areas of eastern France were concerned.

Before criticizing Vidal, one should refer to the time frame during which his work was produced. Towns had not become the powerful regional poles which they are today. And Marxist critics oversimplify Vidal's work, in so far as historical materialism does not deal with local history, environment, or culture but only with the economic substratum. The Vidalian regional approach was quite fruitful; it still is, even though its methodology is now obsolete. Vidal's structuralist approach remains the necessary conduit to any type of geographic reflection.

French geography originally included three branches: physical geography, human geography and regional geography. The geographic region was the founding paradigm, indeed the crowning of geography through synthesis. The *genre de vie* represented a fundamental backdrop to human activities – as such, the first step toward cultural geography. French geographers gave much thought to the concepts of place and milieu, emphasizing the fact that a place has naturalistic, historical and cultural dimensions. A place cannot exist without the human beings who live in it, perceive it and appropriate it for themselves; in contrast, the natural environment exists independently. French geographers also studied population densities and their distribution.

American cultural geography

The first half of the twentieth century saw the evolution of two antagonistic schools of geographic thought in the United States.

- One school, highly pragmatic and focused on economic models, was born in the universities located in the Midwest, in the heart of the America of pioneers.

In this new country, European concepts were irrelevant. Landscape was not culturally differentiated. The physical environment could be widely delineated but did not allow for 'natural regions', as was the case in Europe. Pioneers had turned the past into a *tabula rasa*; Amerindian space had vanished. There remained an unlimited and monotonous space, an area showing no internal differentiation. That which differentiated space was its use, its function, the products which it gave rise to, be they agricultural or industrial. Hence the economic landscape was a key factor. It was organized according to producing areas, communication axes and urban poles. In essence, the differentiated development of space created regions or *belts* based on monoculture and the optimal use of space: dairy belt in the northeast, corn and soya bean belt in the centre of the Midwest, spring wheat belt in the northwest, winter wheat belt in the southwest, cotton belt in the south, tobacco belt in the southeast, and so forth. Towns were both transportation hubs and industrial centres that eventually expanded into industrial belts and various concentric circles of economic activities.

Here was a new way to dissect space into regions that were inherently functional rather than historical or cultural. Space was perceived according to its economic potential. In philosophical terms, this vision corresponded to functionalism.

This type of geography belonged to a new country directed toward market forces and whose values were utilitarian. The Midwestern school did not pay much attention to cultural and historical aspects of landscape, or to the inner organization of geographic spaces. Intellectually narrow, it was nevertheless scientifically sound: it generated fine investigations based on land surveys and maps of potential or actual land use.

- The Berkeley school flourished as a reaction to this materialistic vision. Its founder was Carl Ortwin Sauer (1889–1975), a professor at the University of California at Berkeley, who originated a line of thought that marked the true beginning of American cultural geography.

Sauer was the son of German immigrants to the Midwest. Trained in the school of economic landscape, Sauer soon realizes the limitations of the functionalist approach. He reads Ratzel and *Landschaft* geographers and initiates a dialogue with a cultural anthropologist, Alfred L. Kroeber. Sauer rebels against the reign of economic geography, with its vision of the world locked in a pattern of production belts. In his eyes, such productivistic determinism is much more dangerous than the pseudo-determinism of the natural environment. The best form of anti-determinism is culture, for culture is the very essence of unpredictability. Cultural freedom is infinite by comparison with economic rule.

Carl Sauer criticizes the cliché about necessity being the mother of invention. There is no such thing as determinism ruling over inventiveness, because *inventiveness is the daughter of culture*. Inventiveness does not spring up where expected; it follows complex spatio-temporal diffusion processes that cannot be explained through simple determinism. For example, although rice cultivation is linked with high population densities, it has not been 'invented' to feed large numbers of people. On the contrary, rice cultivation, once discovered, has then allowed for high population densities.

Sauer reads the works of Vidal de la Blache and Jean Brunhes, from which he gathers the concept of *genre de vie*. Sauer sees geography as *the imprint of* genre de vie *onto landscape*. The concept of culture keeps its American connotation, however: culture is understood in its widest sense as *the entirety of human experience*, i.e. spiritual, intellectual and material experience. Cultural geography at Berkeley is now complete. It resembles Vidal de la Blache's definition of human geography.

Sauer and his students carry out field research in tropical areas. They are more intrigued by Latin and Central America than the United States (is this a determining factor?).

Sauer's article, 'The Morphology of Landscape', published in 1925, marks the emergence of cultural geography.[12] On the strength of its unique master, a kind of American Vidal de la Blache, the Berkeley school progressively reaches the rank of the German and French schools.

The five major themes of cultural geography as per the Berkeley school are as follows:

Humans as dwellers

First and foremost, understanding human beings means understanding the environment which they inhabit. Inhabiting a space implies transforming it; by doing so, human beings humanize themselves as they humanize their space.

From this principle derives the need to study the role of humankind in altering natural environments so as to develop their potential and their resources. In his dazzling epic works, Sauer goes back to the dawn of humanity as he investigates the joint history of humans and natural environments. This joint history explains the shaping of landscapes.

Landscapes as cultural imprints

Humans create landscapes when they make use of the ecological setting. Landscapes then become the imprint of a given culture.

Since prehistorical times, human beings have kept on affixing such imprints on the environment as they select plants and animals, as they clear land and erect buildings. Culture is the major agent of nature's transformation and therefore more important than any

climatic change that may occur. Cultural geography thus postu-
lates anti-determinism. From the origins of humanity, men and
women 'determine', 'produce' their environment rather than the
other way around. Further, humans do not construct their environment only in a productivistic perspective; they do so on the basis
of their values and representations.

Cultural geography is interested in *reconstructing the evolution of
landscapes* so as to elucidate their origin. For instance, today's
North American prairie is not the original landscape; far from dis-
playing 'natural' vegetation, it is the outcome of fires set by Native
Americans. Andrew Clark (1949) investigates a similar type of
evolution in the South Island of New Zealand. European settlers
introduced predators – rabbits in particular – that drastically modified local ecology, transformed earlier by the Maori. At the
beginning of the twentieth century, the then-novel concept of
humans as ecological actors displaced the impact of natural causes
as primary explanation for landscape. Today, this concept is relevant again owing to the growth of conservationist and ecological
movements.

Visible cultural elements

To Sauer and his students, culture is *a pattern of interconnected cultural traits*. What is a cultural trait? It is a specific cultural element,
material or non-material, that can be isolated and therefore investigated. A behavioural trait, the usage of a tool, a basic practice
(wine, whisky, or *kava* drinking)[13] are all cultural traits that can be
studied in terms of their originality and their diffusion from a specific hearth.

To analyse a culture one needs to delineate the cultural traits that
comprise it. In this respect Carl Sauer differentiates *visible elements*
from *invisible elements*. Visible elements are linked with the material
aspects of civilizations; they can be read in the landscape, where
they play the role of *markers* that define the first level of culture
areas.

Visible cultural traits are one particular expression of a global culture. For example, a culture of animal breeders is made up of techniques, tools and goods – such as husbandry techniques, roaming areas, a specific habitat (e.g. tents), a specialized type of production (milk among the Masai, cheese or yogurt among Indo-Europeans, hides). These visible elements are connected with specific values, beliefs and rituals. Such is the case of the island of Réunion, in the Indian Ocean, where French settlers, who have fled the large sugar plantations on the coast and moved to the Cilaos Hills, produce three specialties: wine, lentils and embroidery. Any other group would have selected different markers. In their place, just imagine German or British settlers …

As cultural markers, visible elements allow for the study of cultural evolution in space and time, which led Carl Sauer to investigate diffusion processes. Cultural geography tracks the diffusion of practices or tools as well as the borrowing of techniques among human groups: together, they fashion landscapes and delineate culture areas. Hence Sauer's *theory of diffusion* through the migration of cultural traits gives historical breadth to cultural factors.

By investigating the artefacts that survive in landscapes and bear witness to the past, one may reconstitute the differential propagation of an element from its cultural hearth. One example is Lapita pottery in Oceania, the mark of a widespread culture that flourished from 4000 BCE to the beginning of the current era. Members of the Lapita cultural group included canoe sailors, fishermen and breeders of sacred pigs, who came originally from Asia and settled in the South Pacific. Their geographical journey can be traced thanks to fragments of pottery.

Geographers from the Berkeley school have published a number of fine works in this respect, such as an analysis of the spatial diffusion of the blowpipe from a single hearth (which has been rediscovered). Their research on American pioneer life is also well known. Early European settlers left concrete marks of their presence, some of which are still visible in today's landscape.

Geographic aspects of invisible culture

Geographers have neglected this field, which remains open to research and exploration.

Languages, belief systems, customs and religions weave links between humans; these links leave a material trace. Landscape then becomes the matrix of identity as well as its imprint.

Invisible cultural traits create areas of preferential communication among speakers of the same language, heirs to the same history, or followers of a faith. Cultural traits are often rendered into very visible signs, such as toponymies and *geosymbols* that mark out a territory with an array of significant monuments, statues, wayside crosses (e.g. in Brittany), pigeon houses (in the southwest of France), etc.[14] Rather than the function, the sign itself is important. Cultural groups mould their landscapes – not in order to produce more optimally but to express their faith and values. Every culture creates the geosymbols that sustain its identity.

Invisible cultural traits often exert a strong influence over the modalities of spatial occupancy, such as taboos (cf. sacred woods in Africa and mountains in Asia) or food preferences and proscriptions (cf. the absence of pigs in Muslim lands).

Geosymbols and cultural traits, either visible or invisible, are correlated with each other. They merge into *cultural ensembles*, rooting themselves into a territory from which they can spread out. The goal of cultural geography is to understand their diffusion and spatial patterns.

Cultural geographers favour field monographs. The study of a geographic territory allows for a cultural synthesis based on the investigation of *genres de vie*, material features, beliefs, identity, the history of various groups, and other factors along the lines of the culture/landscape binomial. The Berkeley school carried out most of its masterful research in Latin America, investigating tribes or cultural groups in the manner of anthropologists. Researchers in other disciplines admired these magnificent syntheses that led to the concept of culture area. Carl Sauer trained an entire generation of geographers in what, in contrast with economic landscape studies, has been called *cultural landscape studies*.

The Sauerian approach defines *culture areas*, which are coherent and autonomous aggregates related to a certain type of landscape and separated by cultural boundaries. Metaphorically speaking, culture areas look like islands while the world resembles an archipelago of cultures. For example, Latin America is divided into four culture areas: Andean, circum-Caribbean, tropical forest and marginal. As for the African continent, it is split into four areas characterized by bows, spears, clearings and storehouses respectively (Frobenius 1952).

Conclusion

The founding father of American cultural geography delineated *a geography of milieux* with an analytical focus on the environmental characteristics of human societies.

Strictly speaking, this type of geography was not social science. Carl Sauer was interested in the influence of cultures on the material aspects of landscape. The history and geography of cultural traits were only valuable in so far as they shaped landscapes, outlined discontinuities and created culture areas. Sauer did not reflect on the individuals who lived in certain landscapes and had an affective relation with them. The meaning of place was better left to ethnologists: it was definitely not a topic of interest to Sauer.

Carl Sauer imparted great scientific exactness to cultural geography, thereby facilitating the subsequent renewal of the German and French schools. American cultural geography was not an autonomous field of research, but a pivot through which information gathered by neighbouring disciplines was interpreted and synthesized within the framework of geography. American cultural geography was acknowledged as the most global and widely encompassing part of human geography.

According to Sauer, a cultural geographer must have '*a fresh eye and a knowledgeable mind*'. He or she must show a certain mistrust of ideologies, focus on concrete reality and facts rather than signification, and appreciate the singular and complex nature of cultural phenomena. This type of approach does not breed ivory-tower theoreticians; its theories and models are always developed with circumspection. For Carl Sauer (1925), a healthy science is founded on discovery, verification, comparison and output: its object will be determined by its capacity to organize material.

Sauer's disciples founded *cultural ecology*, which sees humans and society as coextensive with ecology. Cultural ecologists are interested in the physiological adaptation of humans to the environment, the effect of the environment on the human organism, and the environmental impact of specific techniques. Human beings are part of an ecosystem rather than its external masters. With cultural ecology humans are not separate from nature: they are seen as a natural species. Often considered as neo-evolutionist, this position has philosophical and critical implications: progress does not mean imposing human rule over nature but following, respecting and marrying it.

Geography of civilizations and culture areas

Under the aegis of Carl Sauer and partly under the influence of the German lineage, the American school set the premises for the geography of culture areas. This is a very concrete geographic approach focused on the diffusion of cultural traits. Maps in this context focus on spiritual and material facts, for instance, the distribution of taro and yam cultivation in Vanuatu.

Closely connected with the geography of culture areas is the geography of civilizations, which represents a wide segment of French geography. Its most important researchers are Pierre Gourou (Asia), Xavier de Planhol (Arabic and Islamic world), Pierre Flatrès

(Celtic world), and Olivier Sevin (Indonesia). Xavier de Planhol's latest work deals with drinking customs (1995).

Also linked with the geography of culture areas is historical geography, whose main figures include Jean-René Trochet, Xavier de Planhol (author of *Géographie historique de la France* – Geo-history of France), and Jean-Robert Pitte.[15]

This line of thought has been thoroughly investigated. It accounts for the human mosaic.

Civilization as cultural region

Each civilization can be seen and understood as a cultural region. The cornerstone of civilizations is often a religious culture or a religious ideology. A civilization may also be defined by the diffusion of a number of cultural traits and by their systemic organization. For instance there is a civilization of the ox in Madagascar, created through the organization and linking of cultural traits, be they material (e.g. breeding techniques), social (related to power and kinship), geographic (such as territories, places of rootedness, itineraries, spatial organization), or spiritual (e.g. ancestor cult or cosmological visions).

This geography is based on the study of great civilizations as producers of landscapes and spatial organization systems. Tropical geographers have greatly enriched this approach, which is far from surprising since they, by definition, encounter the '*other*' in the exotic locales where they live and work. These geographers are aware that different cultures engender different spaces.

Geography according to Pierre Gourou

Pierre Gourou was a contemporary of historian Fernand Braudel and belonged to the same intellectual family, with a powerful intelligence and a remarkable ability to synthesize information, along with an unexpected humility. Gourou's doctoral thesis on rice growers in Tonkin (1936) is a masterpiece. He was a professor at Collège de France and Brussels Free University. Out of a colossal body of work, I will point out *La Terre et l'homme en Extrême-Orient* (1972) and *Terres de bonne espérance: le monde tropical* (1982).

Pierre Gourou's work and that of his disciples (Gilles Sautter, Paul Pélissier, Jean Gallais, Jean Delvert and Olivier Sevin among others) are a testimony to the richness of his thought.

For Gourou, human beings shape landscapes, yet they do so within the framework – and as fully fledged members – of a civilization, which itself may be defined as a pattern of techniques and values. *Homo geographicus* is, first and foremost, a being that organizes the world: civilization organizes the major features of the natural environment in order to create a liveable universe. A civilization is a landscape, and vice versa.

Civilization exerts an influence through two kinds of techniques:
- *Production techniques*, such as tools, material techniques and economic reasoning and modalities.
- *Overlay techniques*, which play a part in human relations, communication and various forms of power. They include:
  1 Social organizations: matriarchy, patriarchy, castes, rules of alliance, etc.
  2 Land tenure: undivided or communal property, parcel size.
  3 Economic systems: as a Bushman explains, '*The worst is to give nothing. Gifts allow for peace among people who do not like each other. We give what we have, that's how we can live together*' (quoted in Gourou 1973, 21). Such words imply that the value of gift-giving is higher than the value of profit-making. In effect this amounts to a choice of civilization, a cultural choice from which flow an economic system and a certain type of logic and internal coherence.
  4 Political systems: these can be multiple, along with their spatial settings (involving boundaries and landscapes).

Pierre Gourou emphasizes the variances between civilizations and their transformations throughout history. Some civilizations, such as the Australian aboriginal civilization, are more spiritual than others.

Gourou's work develops several major concepts:

Cultural drift

(1) Civilizations are the product of a cultural and technical drift, a drift that ensues from technical innovation rather than simple evolution. Therefore it is unpredictable.

In some cases, civilizations may vanish because the invention that could have saved them did not eventuate in a timely manner. For example, the Maya were unable to solve the problem of soil erosion resulting from corn cultivation.

Each step is guided by the previous one and can in turn lead to a domain of specialization. One invention leads to another, and so on. The invention of agriculture in Mesopotamia or New Guinea did not occur instantaneously but was set by the accumulation of experimental observations and small increments in knowledge.

For instance, Mediterranean civilizations experimented with bread, wine, goat's cheese, olive oil and linen and wool fabrics. As for the Chinese, they invented rice, tea, soya 'cheese' (tofu), sesame oil, cotton and silk fabrics, the compass, gunpowder, etc.

Contemporary civilization represents a technical drift more than a conscious and directed evolution.

(2) A civilization is also a history in motion. Thus a city is more than a geographic landscape: it is steeped in history. A series of cumulative drifts turn a site into a city's founding spot and make it grow in that particular site. An urban drift is then set in motion through a series of cumulative processes. Paris could have evolved in a location other than Lutetia.[16]

There is no determinism: nothing as such is necessary but everything occurs through processes of 'cultural drift'.

Geographic beings as singular beings

In Gourou's words, landscapes are *'unique beings'* in the sense that they are not exceptions to the rule but always individual cases (Gourou 1973, 185). Hence the importance of local monographs in geography. *'Geographic facts are striking because of their specific originality, not because they follow rules'* (ibid, 338).

Thus there is not just *one* developing world – with one single explanatory cause – but *many* developing worlds involving various combinations of internal and external causes. In this respect Pierre Gourou's work stands in opposition to the positivist school, the 'new geography' in particular, with its emphasis on laws and systems to explain geographic facts.

Gourou is not 'modern'; in fact modern geographers have attacked his work. Gourou himself is rather ironic vis-à-vis intellectual fashions, whatever they may be. In his eyes, the urbanization of most of humanity may be dangerous. Gourou mistrusts political ideologies and is a conservative, albeit an optimistic one. For instance, he does not grieve for the ecological golden age of the origins. Gourou is not one to write *Tristes Tropiques* like Claude Lévi-Strauss but *Terres de bonne espérance: le monde tropical.*[17]

Other tropical geographers

Among Gourou's spiritual heirs Jean Gallais is perhaps one of the most 'cultural'.

Perception of time and space varies among civilizations and cultural groups. Jean Gallais makes the distinction between the discontinuous, partitioned space of non-modern civilizations and that, smooth and homogeneous, of modern civilizations. In this respect the standard space of modernity is linked with the use of the automobile. Gallais also distinguishes between objective distances and affective, structural and ecological distances, thereby defining a type of cultural ecology. Each ethnic or cultural group has its own ways of representing space and living it. To take the example of the delta of the Niger, there does not exist one 'delta space' making up a 'region'. There are as many delta spaces as there are cultural groups that live in the area: the fishermen's delta, the rice growers', the boatmen's, the breeders'. Each group maintains its own *genre de vie* as well as certain social and spatial organization techniques, from which ensue a vision of space, a practice of territory and a specific perception of distances (Gallais 1967, 1984).

Jean Delvert has studied Buddhism as an ideological structure that elucidates the organization of landscape, modes of thought and societies in Southeast Asia (1961). Like Buddhism, Confucianism in China and Korea is a 'wrap-around' religion that structures people and space.

A specialist on Turkey, Xavier de Planhol has researched the role of Islam in the shaping of landscapes and *genres de vie*. Planhol has also worked on a history of animals and their relation with humans. Planhol is broad-minded in the style of Sauer but has never been interested in initiating a school of thought (1957, 1968, 1993).

Humanistic geography or the geography of representations

This is a newer, more daring aspect of geography. Cultural space is wrought on the basis of representations. In this context cultural space is a space of belief in common values structured by 'iconography' (as per Jean Gottmann's term) and geosymbols. Iconography is both expression and matrix of a people's vision of the world.

Major streams of thought

This geography of identity has been barely investigated as such, although humanistic geography by English-speaking authors and the geography of 'space-as-experienced'[18] by Armand Frémont represent two lineages that have focused on this line of thought. Both lineages aim at charting travel behaviour and investigating mental maps, often on the basis of literature and cinematography.[19]

The most representative figures of humanistic geography are David Lowenthal, Anne Buttimer, Yi-Fu Tuan and Gunnar Olsson as well as French geographers Paul Claval, Augustin Berque and this author. This type of research necessitates a strong reflective component (or some form of field study) or else there is a high risk of finding oneself on the wrong track. Let us also mention the school of *geopoetics* with Kenneth White and the Quebec school with Eric Waddell, Luc Bureau and Jean Morisset. This lineage has strengths but has also made some wrong turns – that of geopoetics, in particular.

According to the humanistic line of thought, the *representation* of a geographic being that societies and individuals craft for themselves is more important than the real thing itself; more exactly, this real object only exists through its representation. Representation refers to iconography, images, beliefs and values.

One contemporary example concerns economic development and its representations. Development is more than a straightforward concept; it is often envisaged as a paradigm that demands immediate action. Yet it is also quite controversial, as the stalled development of the South along the lines of the Western model indicates.[20] The works of Serge Latouche[21] raise the issue: does Westernization mean progress or destitution for populations and cultures worldwide?

Another example of representation concerns tropical Australia, which, as such, does not exist. Aborigines knew how to take advantage of that environment, whereas white Australians found it repulsive – much too different from old England and too close to Asia, with its threatening masses. In the nineteenth century, the 'white man' was deemed physically unable to live and work in tropical environments, which were then considered unhealthy. Therefore the British started to build the Australian nation in the southeastern corner of the continent, where the climate is oceanic, humid and cool. Today, however, Asia is becoming more attractive economically and nearby tropical Australia is developing.

The two opposing forces as per Jean Gottmann

Jean Gottmann is relatively unknown in France because most of his works were published in the United States (1947). The larger part of his research deals with two major themes: (1) the geography of circulation, which investigates flows, movement and modernity, and (2) the geography of iconography, i.e. the cultural images that are embodied in territories, seen as vehicles for identity.

Gottmann examines the partitioning of the world, in other words, the geographical divisions of space. In his view, two bundles of opposing forces animate geographic space: circulation and iconography (or iconology).

- *Circulation* de-partitions space, opening it up for the best and for the worst through the churning together of individuals, goods and ideas. It engenders universalism and cosmopolitanism. Circulatory movement brings about changes in the organization of the world, regions and nations. We are currently living in an era of generalized circulation.
- *Iconography* resists movement and partitions space. This force, which is more abstract than material, rests on identity and symbolic links. Gottmann defines iconography as *'a pattern of elements of a cultural nature that make up the unity of a people'*. Through their iconography, groups share the same representations, visions of the world and values, uniting them within

common spaces of belief. More than ideology, iconography creates stable identities and helps to maintain these identities by resisting generalized circulation and by partitioning geographic space.

Icons are usually defined as holy images, both expressions of a creed and religious objects. Each country or group has its own. Regionalism rests on the unity of its iconography.

Rather than iconography, I prefer the term *iconology* as used in art anthropology, because of its focus on meaning. Icons carry a meaning, which they bestow on those places where they provide roots to a people[22] – and also on the world as a whole, which they make intelligible. Icons offer an image of the world as much as an image of the individual self in the world: they are a worldview from a particular standpoint, a deeply rooted vision.

The circulation/iconology dialectic

The circulation/iconology dialectic facilitates the understanding of many of the tensions and controversies currently occurring worldwide: opening vs. closing, universalism vs. localism, cosmopolitanism vs. isolation, etc.

Plato thought that a political community could only blossom if it remained secluded within its own territory, protecting itself from foreign influence or any force that could engulf it. He advocated small states that were sealed off, well balanced, safe within their boundaries and based on protection rather than communication and equilibrium rather than expansion. History did not comply with Plato's vision.

In contrast, Aristotle favoured an unenclosed, expanding Greece. Alexander the Great fulfilled that mission, creating a vast empire based on sea-borne trade and economic growth within a pluralist system, i.e. a space structured by a network of core cities.

States, nations and regions fluctuate between Plato and Aristotle as they go through various stages. The United States today is Aristotelian; the World Trade Organization (WTO) stands for generalized circulation, the dismantling of economic boundaries and free-exchange policies. Today this inclination brings about sharp reactions. European nations are balancing between the need to build a greater entity and the resistance of established national iconographies. Europe can only succeed if it constructs a global iconology that gives meaning to its region-based composition and allows it to 'resist' circulation flows.

The circulation/iconology dialectic brings forth issues of scale as well; in this respect iconology unifies as much as it insulates. Jean Gottmann's approach delineates the foundation of political geography (involving boundaries/frontiers/regions) and cultural geography (involving iconology), with a particular emphasis on the linkages between the two aspects.

In concrete terms, the study of iconography leads geographers to visualize space as a theatre stage with actors: it is the task of researchers to unveil the meaning of the play. Each actor is associated with personal factors such as beliefs, myths and life history. Hence the geography of actors and representations must call on biographical narratives, literature, movies, interviews and the like. This type of cultural geography can be epitomized by a geography of actors, with the key element being the issue of meaning.

To sum up, this approach allows for the study of culture as a tool that structures communities. Culture does so by determining the rules of group membership and the distinctions between groups. Culture joins as much as it divides; it is linkage as much as differentiation. Scale always intervenes: what unites at one scale may divide at another. Cultural geography thus looks at the construction of collective identities and their spatial 'territories'. That may actually be its main objective. In the final analysis, the relevance of culture to the investigation of the contemporary world is what cultural geography needs to explore. This approach calls on symbols and emotions as much as on facts and reason. It also finds nourishment in other human and social sciences (history, economics, anthropology, etc.). And finally it may resort to literature, testimonies and intellectual meandering just as much as it deals with numbers and material objects. The task is wide-ranging and somewhat unusual.

Cultural space: icons and geosymbols

A geosymbol is a spatial indicator, a sign in space that mirrors and shapes identity. It may be a holy place (Jerusalem or Rome), a highly visible place (the White House in Washington DC, a mountain, a monument), or a sacred place (cf. the role of oak trees, sacred springs, woods and roadside crosses in Brittany). Geosymbols mark out a territory by means of signs, which establish an iconology on the ground. Therefore geosymbols indicate the boundaries of a territory; they also animate it, give it meaning, and structure it. A geosymbol can become the mainstay of a place or site (e.g. Venice, Mont Saint-Michel, St Jacques of Compostella) from which strength will then emanate. These places or sites express a common set of values, which in some cases are the source of pilgrimages. Similarly, pre-Columbian geosymbols bear witness to the communication between heaven and earth. Thus, as symbols and values, geosymbols produce and construct territories.

The marrying of icons and geosymbols creates a cultural (and political) territory and, at a more general level of aggregation, cultural spaces.

In order to comprehend the nature of cultural space, geography must take into account several factors, including cultures as such, values, belief systems and founding myths. Cultural space, which is the foundation of territory, is not a vaguely defined superstructure in that regard. It is the basis of human space. Each region and each political or cultural system is based on a dynamic cultural space that is relatively closed or open.

Cultural space and geosymbols

The various religious and moral values that lay the foundation of a culture rely ordinarily on a discourse and, within traditional societies, on a corpus of myths and traditions [...]. In Australia as in Oceania, cultural representation and the interpretation of myths also lead to a 'sacred geography', which is woven through a web of 'holy places' [...]. Within the geography of the places visited by the civilizing hero, the saint, or the guru, the paths he has followed and the sites where he has revealed his magical power weave a symbolic spatial structure that shapes and creates a territory.

The cultural approach leads us to investigate the concepts of culture, ethnicity and territory. This process helps us delineate a new space, that of geosymbols. A geosymbol may be defined as a place, an itinerary, or an area which, for religious, political, or cultural reasons, takes on a symbolic dimension in the eyes of certain societies and ethnic groups, thereby comforting them within their identity.

The space which geographers study is a multi-level construction. The first level corresponds to structural or objective space, the second is space-as-experienced (*l'espace vécu*), and the third, lastly, is cultural space [...].

Out of these three criteria, objective space, or the space of structures, has been investigated the most. Every society arranges and structures an original space according to its aims, functions and technological level. Regions, cores, axes, flows – in brief, a geographic structure – are the outcome of this process [...].

Spatial structure is not [...] experienced identically in all societies. In particular, the individuals and various groups that constitute these societies may experience it in different ways. Space-as-experienced is space as movement (*un espace-mouvement*), to use a term originated by Armand Frémont.

This type of space is formed by all the places and itineraries that are familiar to a group or an individual. It is a space which they acknowledge, a space associated with daily life. However, this daily and subjective space, although linked with a specific status and social behaviour, does not necessarily correspond to a 'cultural space' and even less to a territory.

Indeed, culture includes the experience of life as much as it transcends that experience. Cultural representation is situated beyond day-to-day activities; sensibility and the search for meaning bring it forth [...]. Reflecting on culture leads one to investigate the role of symbolism in space. Symbols become more intense and vivid when they are embodied in specific places. Cultural space is a geosymbolic space laden with emotions and meanings: in its strongest expression, it becomes a sanctuary-like territory, that is to say, a space of communion with an ensemble of signs and values [...]. The importance of cultural space is not only military or tactical; the fall of sanctuaries and capitals in the course of warfare has always provoked moral upheaval in those who were submitted to it, out of proportion with their actual strategic value [...].

An ethnic group may not be able to survive without a territory, in other words, without roots that allow it to give a foundation to its geosymbols and solidify the space-as-experienced with which it is familiar [...]. The space of geographers thus unfolds along successive levels of perception, not unlike the approach of psychologists who distinguish between different levels of human consciousness [...].

J. Bonnemaison, 'Voyage autour du territoire', *L'Espace géographique*, special issue on cultural geography, 10: 4 (1981), 249–62.

The pioneers of cultural space

This field is expanding rapidly. Some of its forerunners were Albert Demangeon and André Siegfried in particular.

Siegfried (1913, 1952) investigated the long-lasting boundaries between Protestants and Catholics in France. He also studied the manner in which beliefs and myths permeate political identities. Siegfried spoke of the American mythos, or the mythos of New Zealand.

I think that there is such a thing as the French mythos or the Australian mythos. Is there a European mythos, however? On that account, here is what Jean Monnet said about the construction of Europe: '*If I had to do it again, I would start with culture*'.[23]

Tropical geographers often focus their research on cultural space: generally speaking, it is easier to investigate cultures other than one's own.

Space-as-experienced vs. cultural space

What is space besides being a region, an organized system, a structure, or a model? Space is also a subjective experience, which varies according to one's social class, type of employment, or cultural identity.

Cultural space differs from one's subjective experience or perception of space. In fact there may be a discrepancy or even total disconnection between the two. When the two spaces coincide, however, there is strong attachment to place, love of country and territory, and strong patriotism. When cultural space, affective space and space-as-experienced coincide, happiness is the hallmark of a people's collective history.

To analyse the experience of space we can use various methods such as literary texts, dialogues, biographical narratives and surveys. Armand Frémont adopted this approach in his pioneering study *La Région, espace vécu* (1976), which outlines various types of subjective spaces. For example, Madame Bovary's space is small and restricted – the space experienced by Flaubert's heroine is one of frustration but to which is appended a space of dreams and myths. In contrast, the space experienced by working-class couples in the suburbs of Caen, a small town in Normandy, is network-like, dissociated and split among various places associated with work, home, leisure activities, family, and so forth. The space experienced by an artisan from the harbour town of Le Havre, in the early part of the twentieth century, is neighbourhood-oriented: simultaneously restricted and coherent, his territory is geographically limited yet warm-hearted and convivial.

Space-as-experienced includes familiar places (*genres de vie*) as well as places that are acknowledged, loved (or rejected), perceived and represented. Literary and artistic sources are invaluable in this respect. Armand Frémont, for example, owes much to writers Flaubert and Maupassant and to painters of Normandy's landscapes. According to Frémont, '*the fundamental purpose of geography {is} the understanding of the relations of individuals with the places that make up a region*' (1976, 13).

Diasporas and their spaces

Some groups dream of a space other than the one where they currently reside. Their cultural space extends beyond its material container. The actual spaces they inhabit represent exile or refuge; from a cultural standpoint they live somewhere else. Such is the case of Jewish groups that have long lived in Paris or Warsaw rather than in the places that buttress their cultural identity, e.g. Jerusalem, where their geosymbols and iconologies are located.

Spaces of withdrawal

Other groups live in a space that is neutral, unfamiliar and extends well beyond their cultural space – without being outside their own country. That unfamiliar space is not really experienced as such but only travelled through. Although the individuals concerned live in an immense space (involving work, leisure and home), their cultural space is in effect much narrower: e.g. the corner café, family and soccer team. Their cultural space is a shelter, a refuge, a small society in the midst of a space less-travelled – a space that is much larger yet hostile or indifferent to them. Indeed, they are not interested in or even familiar with it.

In the modern world, such spatial schizophrenia creates uneasiness, disharmony and suffering.

The distress of individuals or groups often has a geographical root cause. Such is also the case of adverse historical events.

Space, tourism and leisure

Economic growth combined with increased opportunities of circulation may entail other distorting phenomena. In modern societies, space-as-experienced seems to standardize and undermine cultural space. In this context, one may travel widely, go everywhere and yet remain 'at home', i.e. in the same place culturally speaking. Indeed modernity tends to make places more banal; airports, hotels and organized international tours all look the same. The alternative is to travel within one's room, one's *terroir*, or one's village.

The scale of space-as-experienced – e.g. whether one travels far and wide or not – has no relation to cultural space. Paradoxically, travelling can close rather than open one's mind, thereby destroying cultural space.

Landscape geography

What is a landscape? A classical definition describes it as the expanse of a land that can be viewed.

Already a recurrent, fruitful theme in geography, landscape is currently getting a new start. It is so trendy that some have spoken of 'landscape geography', a concept that has been roundly criticized: *'Landscape is not a goal in itself but the means to an end'*.[24] In other words, a science cannot be based on a fuzzy concept that relies on description and outward appearance. Yet landscapes are now being reinstated in geography and other disciplines, notably literary studies, urban planning and architecture. One reason may be that landscapes are currently threatened: their end is near, it is said; they are under assault.

Human sciences have rediscovered landscapes, and so has biogeography, an up-and-coming discipline with an all-inclusive approach that will allow physical geography, currently broken down into multiple segments, to become one again. A landscape is *'the concrete, spatial translation of an ecosystem'*.[25] Therefore the functioning of a landscape is that of an ecosystem. In terms of its societal aspects, various modalities are involved, as follows (cf. Pinchemel 1988):

- *The landscape as personal environment* makes up the external framework in one's daily life. It is part of one's personality. A literary example is Normandy for Madame Bovary.
- *The landscape as heritage* belongs to a society's collective memory. Standardization and physical damage constantly threaten this type of landscape.
- *The landscape as resource*: the beauty of certain landscapes is a great selling point for dream merchants.[26]
- *The landscape as identity*: landscapes offer signs that allow human groups to situate themselves in time and space and to identify with a given culture and society. Such is the case of ethnic areas (e.g. Chinatowns). What would China be without Beijing and its Forbidden City, or France without Paris?

'Let us understand that our landscapes, our "pays", and our woods are, no less than our language, the substance of our cultural identity, the foundation of our collective personality.'[27]

Jean-Robert Pitte wrote the classic *Histoire du paysage français* (A history of the French landscape) in 1983.

A landscape combines cultural and natural characteristics that endow a territory with a certain appearance – actually an aggregate of certain recurring features. For instance, there are vineyard, wheat, or sugarcane landscapes.

A region is a cultural garment, the enduring testimony of the labour, beliefs and dreams of a human group. For instance, Tuscany, Provence, Sologne are regions. Yet they are also landscapes, or a combination of various landscapes united by one or several founding characteristics.

Just like a human face, a region has a unique expression that one may perceive, recognize, touch, love, or hate; it is a sensory space made of colours, smells and images … (Béguin 1995).

Geographic landscapes are physiognomies that aggregate the physical and cultural characteristics of a region. In some cases several types of landscape rather than a single one may be involved. One example is the landscape of Limousin (central France), where two types of environment co-exist: mountain and plateau. The mountainous areas of Limousin used to be pastureland, today they are covered with coniferous forests. The bocage-like plateau includes woods and grassland, with farms and hamlets but no large villages. Small towns are located at the junction of plateau and mountainous areas.

A region may associate several landscape images rather than a single image, e.g. High Limousin and Low Limousin, or plateau vs. plain in Lorraine.

Landscapes – urban landscapes in particular – represent an entanglement of various layers where recent configurations do not necessarily obliterate more ancient features. Such is the case of the Latin Quarter or rue Saint-Jacques in Paris.[28]

Augustin Berque has analysed the strength of the human–landscape relation (1984, 1990, 1994, 1995).

Berque posits a major linkage between the identity of human groups and the landscape that permeates their lives and which their forebears have shaped. Berque's topic of inquiry is the bond between Japanese culture and natural environment. This cultural link and source of identity is the landscape (1982, 1986, 1993).

The Japanese have patterned their landscape along the lines of a mountain/plain dyad: mountainous areas are left in a state of wilderness; they are not the domain of humans and therefore are not utilized. Human beings occupy plains, where they create cores of high population density. This approach follows a cultural rationale rather than an environmental one.

Rural and urban landscapes and, at a more intimate scale, gardens and house styles establish Japanese identity and basic personality. It is a way to live space at various levels.

Berque approaches the human–nature relation in philosophical terms: landscape carries meaning; it is both imprint and matrix. Berque thinks that some civilizations are more landscape-oriented than others. For example, the Japanese have turned nature into a landscape where they feel at ease and which they like. Australian aborigines live in the midst of a sacred nature that they do not construct but travel through. The Dreamtime of ancestors exists in parallel to the visible landscape of Australia.

With its icons and geosymbols, a landscape is always a cultural space superimposed over a natural space: it is more or less bountiful, more or less aesthetically pleasing, more or less inherited or modern. It tells much about the civilization that has produced it. Geographers view landscapes as historians view archives: they are a treasure trove of information.

3

On whether culture and civilization are operational concepts in geography

The idea of culture

Is it a residual?

In 1981 the journal *L'Espace géographique* sponsored a debate on the theme of culture. Geographers from various universities and research organizations discussed the role of culture within the discipline. Their views diverged widely. Some participants stated, with much sincerity, that culture is what remains when everything else has been explained. In other words, culture is a residual factor – what remains once other analytical tools have been used, once economic and social geography specialists have looked at a topic, once the 'heavy artillery' of models, concepts and analyses have played their part. This mysterious remnant is what motivates people, what 'makes them run', yet it cannot be measured. Culture is an intangible factor related to human freedom and creativity. Although culture cannot be reduced entirely to rational analysis, this does not mean that one should discard intelligent thinking in order to understand cultural phenomena.

Let us take trees as an example. Why is there deforestation in the highlands of Madagascar? Geographers can analyse this process methodically. In the same vein, we can examine perception and representations of drought in the northern part of Australia.

In the early 1980s, geographers saw culture as the last intervening factor or as something which could not be otherwise explained. For instance, how does one characterize the distribution of suicides, alcoholism, or fertility rates in France? Why is there rugby in the southwest of France? Why do 80 per cent of high-school graduates in New Caledonia originate from Lifou Island?

Thus culture has been defined, for the most part, as what remains 'unfiltered' at the very end of a 'scientific experiment'. But what is culture's actual explanatory power? That is the problem. Is culture an ornament or a foundation? Is it a detail in geographical understanding or part of its essence? Cultural geographers, of course, favour the latter view.

Culture is an achievement

The idea of culture is part of our Greco-Roman heritage. The word *culture* derives from the Indo-European *kwel* meaning to bring up, take care of, like, love. Linguists have reconstructed the evolution of the word. Indo-Europeans were horsemen, warriors, and herdsmen who lived in the Steppes. They first used the term in relation to the training of animals, to the breaking-in of horses in particular. The Greeks then used the word in agriculture, in the sense of maturation or ripening of cultivated plants. In ancient Greece culture meant the growth of the mind, its unfolding and the fulfilment of its potential, in the image of a plant whose vital energy must be channelled, controlled and constantly watched over so that it only gives the best of itself. Culture was the outcome of a constructive activity that was neither spontaneous nor 'natural', which, in other words, was far from obvious. It was a human creation, a focus for willpower – the highest as far as mind, knowledge and belief were concerned. Culture constructed itself at the very heart of a civilization, and each generation transferred it to the next. As far as the Greeks were concerned, culture was an achievement.

The word disappeared from Indo-European languages at the time of Barbaric invasions. Significantly, it re-appeared in the French language in the twelfth and thirteenth centuries, at a time when European civilization was entering a phase of renewal. The word had a strong religious connotation: it was synonymous with worship. Culture encompassed the Christian *cult* and allowed human beings to become holier.

During the Renaissance and especially in the eighteenth century, in the age of Enlightenment, the term 'culture' was to take on a larger meaning – equivalent to today's sense of the word. Mind, knowledge and refinement became the province of culture. It implied universal progress and values, making it the opposite of nature, barbarian practices and superstition. In brief, culture represented civilization and the fulfilment of the human spirit, a voluntary creation that was anything but spontaneous. This interpretation of the term was close to the original definition from ancient Greece, but with a less religious connotation.

The etymology of the word culture is important, for it entails a double meaning and an ascending course from the inferior order of nature to the superior order of the mind. Culture rests on the duality – matter and spirit – of human beings and their action:
• Culture unveils the inward action of human beings to construct themselves;
• It reveals their outward action in and upon the world to construct their environment.

Both cases involve developing a domain that would otherwise remain barren or wild and giving it meaning. This idea decreases the gap between innate and acquired factors; it minimizes the nature/culture duality. Such duality is artificial since the two aspects co-exist in human beings.

Culture and social science

In the pragmatic view of American geographers, all features that are not connected with nature are related to culture. It is the global human experience – what French geographers call 'human geography', albeit with a more restricted meaning. On a map, American geographers identify what is 'natural' (soil, hydrology, vegetation, relief, etc.) and what is 'cultural' (houses, paths, fields, crops, etc.). In other words, a geocultural feature represents what human beings have created. As such, it is a visible feature that can modify an environment. This type of feature is anthropic:[1] it delineates the humanized landscape.

Culture is at the very heart of the discipline of ethnology. Each ethnic group is identified by a specific culture, a highly complex pattern that must be understood as a whole. Any individual born in a society participates in a culture. Culture is collective and always refers to a community, be it a clan, a society, or the like. Herodotus said, 'Custom is the king of all things'. To understand the custom that brings individuals together is to understand these individuals.[2] Basic needs are innate and universal, but the method to fulfil those needs may vary: there are many ways to feed oneself, sleep, be sheltered, or work. A culture meets universal needs through its own original creation, which is an arrangement of acquired and learned behaviours and attitudes. In this respect the 'cultural breaking-in' of children links back to the Greek definition of culture. This arrangement of behaviours and mental attitudes makes up a system wherein all elements uphold each other, like an organic structure.

Ethnologists often describe cultures as holistic systems according to which each aspect can only be understood in relation to the whole. The holistic standpoint stands in contrast with analytical methods: one accounts for a feature by integrating it into the whole to which it belongs. For example, Melanesian land tenure can only be understood through its relationship with the leadership system, the kinship system and the agrarian system, and reciprocally.

Paradoxically, however, ethnologists have long used self-enclosed, 'bunker-like' monographs and have often avoided investigating the possible links between different cultures. Yet any culture communicates with others, even to a very small extent. In geography especially, one must not confine oneself within the discipline but work on its margins occasionally and borrow forms of knowledge or methods from other sciences.

According to the cultural viewpoint, all cultures are different from each other while being similar in certain aspects; that is, they meet common needs and goals in distinctive ways. Each culture represents a local variation on universal themes. Cultures create the diversity of the world, thereby making it more interesting. At one level differences separate; at another they are a gathering force.

Linguists give a definition of culture that is perhaps the clearest and most thorough. This is hardly surprising. After all, is there anything more cultural, synthesizing, constructed and symbolic than a language? Here is the definition spelled out by Emile Benveniste, a linguist who is a specialist of Indo-European languages: '*I call culture the human environment – everything that, beyond the fulfilment of biological functions, gives shape, meaning and contents to human life and activity*'.[3] The term *human environment* is essential. It designates the geographic milieu, that is, nature as shaped by culture, in other words symbolic reality and reality as perceived by the senses. The term 'culture' is used here in its material dimension – that of American geography – and in its intellectual and spiritual dimension, whereby culture is a system of attitudes, beliefs and symbols. Linguists rightly say that a language is more than a simple designation of the world; it is also a particular representation of the world, that is, a locally based conception of the world, a view from a particular standpoint that gives meaning to the lives of human beings in that place. Therefore culture must also be understood as the sphere of religions and beliefs. This final level of culture may be the most significant and sensitive since it delineates the largest common denominator. For instance, one speaks of an Islamic culture, a Catholic or Protestant culture. These realities transcend national cultures and are in some circumstances much more influential.

Culture encompasses a wide domain that goes from the prehistoric stone implements that researchers dig up in the field to Buddhist precepts and founding myths, and from kitchen recipes to the most elaborate intellectual constructions, be they ideological or religious. Because of its vastness the cultural domain is somewhat ambiguous. The term *culture* includes material civilization as well as the civilization of the mind. Along these lines, the cultural postulate is that the two are linked and make up a system. In this case one speaks of cultural complex. A culture is somewhat similar to a language; it is a holistic and interactive system; each element evolves interdependently with all others. As a system, culture encompasses the most material feature as well as the most spiritual aspect. Culture represents the movement that goes from one to the other – from a specific way of life to the meaning of life, from flint implements to the existence of God (or its denial).

What is acquired and what is transmitted

Like language, culture is also defined by the fact that it is transmitted. Culture is the aggregate of what human beings inherit from previous generations: representations, knowledge, values, ideas and types of sensitiveness. Culture is also what they invent and what they experience within a given space and time. For instance, there is the culture of the 1930s or the 1960s; the culture of a given region, town, or suburban area; company culture, and so forth. Every generation and every group innovates at the same time as it receives. Every culture reinvents itself. There is no such thing as pure tradition, even for fundamentalists. A new generation or group reinterprets traditions and makes them its own by enriching them with new features or discarding aspects it no longer validates.

A given culture thus remains a living tradition, a mixture of transmitted and acquired traits, a reality in motion. This phenomenon varies to a smaller or greater extent, of course. There are open cultures and closed cultures, evolving cultures and others in an apparent state of inflexibility.

This continuous process of creation – or, more exactly, of recreation – is the foundation of collective identities for local groups, tribes, countries, nations and other social entities. Identities are constantly shifting. They construct themselves; the enriching of their cultures reinforces them; occasionally they become weaker and are no longer involved in a process of construction. Indeed, since cultures live they can also die, a process that always aligns identities in new directions.

Melanesian custom

Custom carries a number of connotations. Within the context of the so-called 'Pacific paradox', the term takes on singular amplitude.[4]

Does custom represent a reality or a strategy? Can it be the basis for nationalism, the necessary conduit to independence?

In South Africa, for example, the nationalism of Zulu kings, based on custom (*Inkata*), used to be at odds with that of the Western-educated, urbanized élite. Similarly, the custom/culture split occurs frequently in developing countries. Custom can be 'manipulated' when it is a matter of the conquest or reconquest of power. In the case of Tanna (Vanuatu), outside interests were involved but local citizens (*Ni-Vanuatu*) were not really manipulated since they were fully aware of their custom. This is the reason why anthropologists found it very difficult to analyse the issue of 'custom's rebels' in Tanna.[5]

Does custom carry its own substance or does it correspond to a set of circumstances? Again, the example of Tanna can shed light on the topic.

Before the New Hebrides reached independence, the island of Tanna witnessed a series of major revolts against European occupiers.[6] Tanna liberated itself culturally before it did so politically. The first Presbyterian missionaries settled in the island in 1860 and attempted to convert the islanders but encountered many difficulties due to local warfare. In 1938–39, the island 'de-converted' from Christianity and returned to paganism. The presence of a mysterious figure called John Frum, a sort of local prophet, made the fight between Catholics and Protestants more convoluted as he heralded the coming of a mythical and ideal era, which contributed to the emergence of a syncretic religion – a blend of Christianity and paganism. In 1940, Tanna entered a phase of cultural uprising and 100 British police arrested John Frum. He was deported to Vila (the capital of the New Hebrides), where he died in exile seventeen years later. During these seventeen years there was an intense repression against Tanna's neo-pagans and a dramatic decrease in the island population. Far from eradicating paganism, British repression made it more forceful.

After the New Hebrides (renamed Vanuatu) gained independence, pagan custom was used as a strategy to reconquer the political power bestowed by the British. In the name of custom, supporters of tradition rebelled against their fellow citizens who held power at the national level and whom the Melanesian élite, educated in missionary schools, had put in office.

Is today's custom invented or is it close to traditional custom? What does it represent? What does it entail?

Custom is a claim on the past that is intended to enlighten present issues. Thanks to custom, the islanders remain faithful to the memory of their ancestors. Custom represents a return to the values and mores of long ago, before the present era and the modernity of the West erupted into an age-old way of life. The islanders withdraw within their cultural heritage; it is a return to ancient places, myths and rituals ... a return to the golden age of the origins.

Melanesian culture is experienced every day. It is at odds with the values of 'white', mostly urban, modernity with its cash economy and social demands. The custom of 'Black Men'[7] stops where towns begin. It emphasizes village life and a network of social obligations, mutual help and solidarity. It does not refute the demands of the clan, the links with the land, or the authority of elders and chiefs (or kings in Polynesia). Wishing to escape from such narrow social relationships, which can be oppressive and frustrating, and from the system of indebtedness (a mandatory solidarity that links individuals and interests), some individuals prefer to migrate to urban areas. Custom emphasizes the community rather than the individual, and in this respect the community oppresses the individual as much as it supports him or her by means of village-based networks of reciprocal exchange. In Tanna, the exchange ritual is characterized by dancing and consecrated by the *toka* ceremony. The material gift-giving that occurs between two networks of alliance only bears meaning when it is accompanied by an ancestor-honouring ritual. The aesthetics of the ceremonial dance are more important than the value of the goods exchanged (mostly taro, pigs and young women of marriageable age). The *toka* ceremony thus helps maintain a certain level of social peace.

Custom is an affirmation of cultural and political identity. It tightens links among local residents, asserts the rights of original inhabitants, and fights against alienation by excluding 'foreigners' (i.e. all those who are not 'kin' since a 'foreigner' cannot enter the circle of alliance). Custom often provides a political foundation to new nations or to nationalistic movements that aspire to sovereignty (e.g. in New Caledonia).

Yet this type of engagement is also a dividing factor. Custom expresses a profound otherness, especially when it justifies cultural behaviours that do not abide by Western standards: 'I am acting this way, because this is my custom'. There is a denial of economic rationality as well.

Custom is characterized by a particular space. In Tanna, the dancing places used for the *toka* ceremony are clearings in the forest. Roads of alliance link dancing places together in network-like fashion; they organize a reticulated space and structure social life in its entirety. Traditional villages are located within a web defined by this network of roads and places. Once they have federated a number of villages, two groups of alliance meet at a dancing place for the *toka* ceremony – at least this was the rule until Europeans arrived. Missionaries fractured that space when they set up Christian villages on the seashore, turned to the outside world. All islanders were gathered in those villages. The inland region was abandoned for several decades, although eventually the villagers went back to their customary places and revived the heart of the island. Missionaries also altered traditional social life to a great extent. For instance, disputes among villagers used to concern pigs primarily, then women and land. Under the influence of missionaries, land has become the most frequent source of disputes, followed by women and pigs.

The dancing place

The centre of space and the heart of traditional society in the island of Tanna (Vanuatu)

The mythological construction of Tanna [...] rests on the idea that sacred powers appeared in certain places then spread out through space by means of traditional roads [...]. Myths reveal a society whose two main facets are the concepts of canoe (*niko*) and dancing place (*yimwayim*). The canoe is perceived as the larger unit; it gathers the inhabitants of a territory where all, or almost all, types of social status are represented. In contrast, the dancing place is a more restricted unit corresponding to a small local group that is likely to take on one or, at most, a few categories of social status. Several dancing places (and local groups) make up a canoe; social unity is the result of allegiance towards the dancing place occupied by the most ancient group. [...]

In the final analysis, spatial systems rather than social structures bring the islanders together and make them a 'society'. Organized in terms of hierarchical places and the confluence of routes, Tanna's spatial systems represent a network geography whose basic unit is associated with the concept of *canoe*. The canoe includes three levels of organization, with each level corresponding to a geographic scale. At the upper level is the canoe as such, or *niko* [...]. The canoe's scale is that of the great territory: the country of custom or *ima* [...]. The middle level involves residential groups, which are organized around dancing places (*yimwayim*). Each dancing place gathers several hamlets or kinship segments within the same area of social relation [...] and represents a microterritory of a few dozen acres [...]. Lastly, the lower level involves 'barriers' (*nowankulu*). A 'barrier' is a small hamlet that used to be fenced in; it gathers several households that belong to a patrilineal kinship segment [...]. Each canoe includes a variable number of dancing places. These are linked with one dancing place considered as primal because of its origin and the high level of the social functions associated with it [...]. The site where the canoe 'merges' all its components into one centre is the primeval dancing place created at the time of foundation. Sacredness permeates that dancing place [...]. The first ancestors appeared there, and the great banyan trees that give it shade still bear their names. Magical powers and social functions are rooted in it. A canoe lives thanks to this *great place*, which serves as its heart [...]. By way of contrast, secondary dancing places make up a *profane periphery*; this secondary network arose when the great places of the origin and their powers became spatially segmented. The canoe and the primeval dancing place are identical [...]. The canoe thereby heralds a powerful principle: the unity of place is identical with the unity of the origin. Any and all canoes bear the same identity.

{A description of the Lamlu dancing place follows:}

The canoe of the Nalhyaone spreads out at the heart of Middle Bush.[8] Its unity is rooted in the founding place where the first ancestor, Noklam, brought into existence – or dug out, *pikim,* as one says in Bislama – the primordial dancing place of Lamlu. [...] Noklam arrived in Lamlu, where he began to live, transforming into a man. Noklam engendered a son, Ya'uko, whom he set up in a second dancing place in Lamnatu [...]. Thereafter, these two ancestors engendered other men to whom they gave new names [...] and whom they sent out to create dancing places. By engendering Ya'uko, this other part of himself, Noklam created a 'mimetic partner' – both son and rival with whom he exchanges women and shares the steering of the canoe. Noklan and Ya'uko are the origin of the two initial lineages that share the powers and the main functions of the Nalhyaone canoe [...]. In theory, this clan is endogamous: since it is divided into two inter-marrying lines, it does not need the outside world to reproduce itself [...].

The Lamlu *yimwayim* is located at the intersection of two major roads [...]. The *yimwayim* represents the confluence of routes organized around a central place where inter-marrying segments enter into alliances with each other; it is also a starting point toward external allies located farther away. The dancing place is a founding place as well as a crossroads: it represents a relay node in the chain of relations of alliance. Roads cross the territory and have as much importance as the dancing place itself. Major roads have names and are controlled. To identify himself, a man from Tanna's traditional society names the dancing place to which he belongs and the road to which he is linked [...]. To each of the roads converging toward the dancing place corresponds [...] a *nowankulu* [...] that gathers one or several closely related nuclear families [...]. The *nowankulu* is a household place reserved for women and young children, whereas the *yimwayim* is a social place reserved for men who, at dusk, meet there to drink *kava* together [...].

The spatial model of the dancing place has three components: the site itself, which is a tree-lined clearing with bare soil where custom's rituals occur; the roads [...]; and finally, a little farther away, the 'barriers' or settlement nuclei corresponding to kinship segments [...].

At the time of the origin, the initial group only held the dancing place of foundation. The history of men, their growth in numbers and their rivalry caused the canoes to partition and spread throughout the space of the territory, where they established other dancing places and new settlement nuclei. The ensuing process of fragmentation can threaten the canoe's unity. The ritual aims at recreating the original political unity, which can only be experienced in the founding place.

J. Bonnemaison, *Les Gens des lieux. Histoire et géosymboles d'une société enracinée: Tanna. Les fondements géographiques d'une identité: l'archipel du Vanuatu* (revised edition of *Tanna: les hommes-lieux*), Paris, ORSTOM, 1997, 145–56.

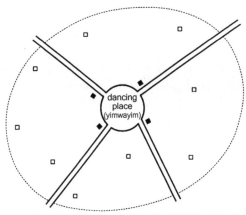

The spatial model of a dancing place

dancing place (yimwayim)

☰ traditional road (suatu)

···· territorial limit of residing group

■ 'barrier' (nowankulu) or original settlement nucleus

□ 'barrier' (nowankulu) or secondary settlement nucleus

The dancing place (*yimwayim*) emerges at the junction of two paths (*suatu*). A hamlet (*nowankulu*) is located along each section of the path; in the past, a protective fence made of reed surrounded it. The 'road' is under the care of the 'barrier'. In the course of rituals, 'barriers' 1 and 3, situated across from each other, join together; 'barriers' 2 and 4 do the same. The four 'sides' of the dancing place are now only two, each being the ritual partner of the other. All 'barriers' located in the depth of the territory are 'secondary barriers' that are linked with one or the other among the four 'founding barriers', which they consider as their original place and to which they answer during rituals.

J. Bonnemaison, *Les Gens des lieux. Histoire et géosymboles d'une société enracinée: Tanna. Les fondements géographiques d'une identité: l'archipel du Vanuatu* (revised edition of *Tanna: les hommes-lieux*), Paris, ORSTOM, 1997, 149.

In Melanesia, custom has founding places. Among those is the dancing place, a geosymbol that epitomizes and expresses the symbolic aspects of culture. In essence, the landscape of the origins is the only one that exists, through the visible landscape superimposed over it. This spatial system expresses a cultural system based on exchange – the flow of information and goods. It makes up a reticulated space since it is not structured by a centre but by a founding place with several interrelated focal points, which themselves do not belong to a hierarchy but are dissimilar. In this case there is spatial *speciation*, i.e. gradual spatial differentiation.[9] Culture cannot live outside its space. Without it, culture loses most of its value.

• Is custom a type of culture addicted to the past?

Does custom represent true nostalgia about the past? Is it characterized by the wish to go back to things as they were? There is faithfulness, undoubtedly, but no real nostalgia. Today, there is as much distance between Melanesians and their past – penis sheaths and canoes – as there is between the French and the horned helmets of their Gallic ancestors.[10] In fact, custom is an idealized reconstruction of the past to serve current political choices better and, in a way, anticipate the future. Through custom the strength of Melanesian identity is affirmed; yet custom is never a simple replication. One should eschew a vision of culture that is attached or addicted to the past; culture is not a relic frozen in a referential space-time. Custom represents *rootedness* within a tradition as much as *movement* and *change*. Far from being a fixed system, it includes heritage and innovation, two factors that are both necessary and complementary. In contrast to Western societies, whose cultural gaze is turned to the present or to ephemeral instants, custom-based movements emphasize the importance of the continuity between faithfulness to the past and anticipation of the future. A people cannot have progress without being linked to its roots, without continuity with its traditions. '*A people without memory is a people without future*', said Nietzsche. This quotation is not far removed from the definition of the word custom as *'progress with the past'*.[11]

Thus, custom (in Melanesia) and authenticity (as it has been called in Africa) stand as political/cultural phenomena that emphasize not the precedence of the past over the present, or that of tradition over modernity, but the link between one and the other. Such phenomena always involve reinvention and reconstruction as well as renewed focus on a certain vision of the past. In turn, this vision brings more strength to the collective ability of a community to face the future and the outside world. A type of syncretism evolves, which blends the old with the new.

The transmission of culture

Cultural transmission involves cultural interaction since, by definition, culture entails communication between those who share that culture. Hence a geocultural area is primarily a communication area.

Communication messages travel along channels and networks that have a spatial component. A culture lives according to the ways it is reproduced and transferred, just as it is modified by the operational aspects of the transmission itself. Today this process involves communication techniques, notably the media. As is well-known, a culture is transmitted through various media but, more importantly, the media themselves transform culture. We then speak of a media-driven culture, or culture as spectacle, which at times takes the place of culture as such – an evolution that is rarely synonymous with enrichment or achievement in the Greek sense of the term.

This approach to culture encompasses (1) *the human milieu, both material and spiritual*; and (2) *a way of life and the meaning of life*. Culture is *at once inherited and reinvented*. It is personal as much as collective – personal because all individuals internalize culture, even when they reject it, and collective because culture is an unconscious collective structure conveyed through the social breaking-in. Culture is also a communication system. It is now being increasingly influenced by modern techniques of representation and transmission. To geographers, the concepts of *milieu*, *identity*, *representation*, *cultural flows* are important, for they imply a *space* of transmission, a *territory* which these factors shape, and an *environment* which they modify.

The idea of civilization

Genesis of the concept

The concept of civilization carries several connotations. While the idea of culture originated in Greece and came to us via the Latin word *cultura*, the word *civilization*, at least in the present sense of the term, is French. It originated in the eighteenth century to designate the antonym of barbarian practices.

The word comes from *civitas*, the city, in the sense of 'conscious and responsible community'. What is 'civilized' is associated with citizens and therefore refers to civil society, to 'civility'. Civility is the art of collective living. Some forms of civility can be very rich and strong while others are less so. Anything that refines social practices is civilized.

Thus civilization has an urban connotation whereas culture, as we have seen earlier, mostly refers to rural societies. The two terms are equally rich and complex yet nevertheless quite different. Civilization concerns towns, citizens, urban communities and, by extension, political matters (*polis*, from which 'political' is derived, was the Greek equivalent of the Latin *civitas*). Culture relates to the development of minds and forms, to the biological and the sacred, to art, nature and the meanings of nature: the term is more religious, more artistic, close to the basic elements of a nature that it sublimates, and linked with perennial metaphysical questions. The relation between nature and culture is an ancient philosophical issue, therefore not fortuitous.

The term *civilization* originated in France, where it attained a great degree of success. It then became widespread throughout Europe. The continent had already characterized itself as an 'Occident' that set the stage for progress. To the concept of culture were now added the notions of development and modernity, which allowed eighteenth-century Europe to delineate a world in motion and oppose a superior culture – its own – to barbarian cultures. Along these lines, the idea of civilization carries philosophical and positive connotations.

Singular/plural

'Civilization' has a dual meaning, depending on whether it is used in the singular or the plural. Civilization, in the singular, is the universal civilization of good and progress. It is identified with the city, the development of technology and knowledge, and the reign of reason, and by extension it represents a value judgment. A civilization is a culture that has become more universal, that has transformed itself on the path of progress.

Civilizations, in the plural, have a different meaning according to each language; at the core the term is very close to culture. Civilizations are major cultures. They represent culture areas that are superior in terms of vision and extent; they are 'successful' cultures, so to speak.

Definitions

Dictionaries define civilization as '*the total pattern of religious, moral, cultural, social and material features that characterize a country or a society*'. French dictionaries define culture more narrowly than civilization: culture is limited to intellectual knowledge and learning processes ('*Culture is what remains when one has forgotten everything*', according to Edouard Herriot).[12] Culture is seen as the sum total of the intellectual aspects of a civilization. This notion corresponds to the Marxist-defined superstructure.

Culture, civilization, culturalism and universalism

- Culturalism and universalism

There is no universal culture, only a variety of cultures set in time and space. These are occasionally closely related although often markedly different. Culture is a view of the world, set somewhere in the world.

The plurality of cultures enriches humankind. Does that fact challenge the myth of a universal civilization or a universal reason, as Kant posited in his *Critique of Pure Reason*? The debate between culturalism and universalism rages on today.

- The Marxist definition

As an ideological superstructure, culture is dependent on the material and economic structure of society. Culture helps to reproduce and preserve this structure by getting minds accustomed to the conventional values that culture holds. In brief, culture shapes minds in terms of the dominant ideology.

In the counter-discourse of neo-Marxists, the cause-and-effect order is reversed: one can act upon the material and economic structure by acting upon the superstructure. A case in point is Mao Tse-tung's Cultural Revolution in China.

According to the cultural-power theory of Gramsci (1891–1937), power is gained through the subversion of minds – through counter-culture. This is the theory of the 'cultural hegemony of the proletariat'. Ideological and cultural majority precedes political majority in most cases.[13]

- Civilization as a form of the universal

Culture and civilization refer to two distinct historical and geographical traditions.

To the French and the English, culture represents the total pattern of moral and intellectual traditions that create a civilization – civilization being a higher artistic and literary aspect of it. At the time of the Enlightenment, in the age of Diderot and Rousseau, civilization is an all-inclusive concept; in other words, culture partakes of civilization. Civilization is the end result of an extensive cultural unfolding. It is synonymous with orderly social values. Civilization refers to the idea of progress and to all that is most recent and modern.

Civilization is universal. It is a gathering force, making itself available and open to the world. Civilization can be quantified, measured. A civilization can become global; it is spoken of in the singular and referred to as a state of civilization. For example, the USA upholds the American civilization. French culture also endorses the mythos of civilization; the French see their culture as a civilization with universal leanings. This explains why the French have carried out holy wars, as with Joan of Arc or the revolutionary government of 1793–94.[14]

Civilizations tend to convey the idea that they hold universality and truth for all and that they represent the model that others must follow. The French define their civilization as the universal form of Truth or as universal Reason; the Americans define theirs as the universal form of Good.[15]

- Cultures as forms of difference

In reverse, the German tradition defines *Kultur* as superior, whereby culture expresses local rather than global concerns and refers to the particular, the subjectivity of communities, and what makes them different. Culture is the soul of a people. One does not enter it; one is born in it and inherits it. Hence the scope of culture is stronger and also more restricted. Italy or Germany are culture-based rather than civilization-based. Civilization gathers; culture differentiates. Civilization-oriented countries are ethnocentric and reject differences. Culture-based peoples exalt differences; by respecting differences one can reach universal values. In a famous speech (1807), Fichte spoke of the German people '*born to the world through its language*' – a people that rebelled against the civilization that the French wanted to impose on them.

The same debate raged on during World War I, when the Allies claimed to fight for the cause of universal civilization against the Barbarians of central European empires, addicted to the past and regressive. The Germans fought in the name of their culture or, in the words of Thomas Mann, for '*the possibility itself of a culture*'.

• Culture vs. civilization

Oswald Spengler differentiates between culture – as soul, life, creativity – and civilization – as intellect, reason and analysis. The latter represents the unavoidable fate of any culture and thus its death (Spengler 1931–33). A culture is in the image of a plant: its high times are those of birth and youth, when the sap of innovation springs up from within. A civilization represents the ripening of the plant: entropy takes over, progress and technology win over spiritual creation. There is discontinuity and irreversibility among cultures when they find themselves in a creative mode. In contrast, civilizations gather decayed cultural forms.

The concept of civilization in the human sciences

Within the social sciences, such as anthropology, history and geography, the term of culture is understood in a much wider sense. Culture and civilization are spoken of in the plural. The concept of culture involves two levels: it includes material values and spiritual values, matter as much as mind. Hence a certain confusion – and an apparent contradiction in terms.

For ethnologists or cultural geographers, that is, for social scientists dealing with culture, there is no superior culture or civilization as such, but a plurality of cultures and civilizations that contribute to the richness of humankind. There may be relations of force among them, which engender circumstantial inequalities: such is the game of history, but no culture or civilization possesses a superior substance to which the others should convert, so that these relations change with the context. In this sense, Australian Aborigines were superior to the British settlers who found themselves near starvation in nineteenth-century Port Jackson.

• Differences in scale

Culture and civilization differ, not in terms of their inherent characteristics, but in terms of their respective scales. A civilization carries a wider meaning and spatial extent. In essence, civilizations are 'large-sized'; they are inclusive cultures that are spread over broad, fairly unchanging spaces and that often aim at the universal. For example, Western civilization involves Western Europe and North America. There are also Amerindian civilizations, Islamic and Indian civilizations, and so forth. Each of these civilizations includes an indeterminate number of cultures and cultural systems.

Civilizations construct and synthesize the collective characteristics that make up the great cultural and geographical patterns of humankind. Thus, a civilization is always a society, an economy, a culture, a history, a collective mentality and somehow a synthesis of all these aspects. A civilization is a great socio-politico-cultural and economic aggregate. When defined as the common values shared by the majority, culture represents civilization's most essential binding agent, that through which the total pattern holds. Culture is the source of civilizations, not their totality.

A civilization is to be apprehended at a very small geographic scale and in a long-term perspective. This approach spans societies over the course of long stretches of time and perceives them within their most extensive spatial reach. The great length of time and the spatial extent that characterize a civilization are also what differentiate it from a culture, which refers more to groups, life-as-experienced and daily aspects. We understand civilization at the macro-societal level and in the meta-cultural dimension; in contrast, we comprehend culture at the micro-level of ethnic, national, or regional cultures.

A civilization always claims to be universal. It carries a message of dominance and has a stake in hegemony. It is armed with a civilizing mission. This can lead to some problems. Are we headed toward a collision course between civilizations? Although cultures co-exist, civilizations are often less tolerant. In brief, cultures carry on a dialogue whereas civilizations fight each other. This fundamental issue is a distinguishing factor of our times.

Cultural geography is the study of both cultures and civilizations. At the core, the process involved is cultural in both cases but the scale differs from one to the other.

4

The cultural system

A cultural system includes a number of core themes and is characterized by a specific internal organization.

The cultural approach in geography means that one is studying a holistic system, the major components of which cannot be dissociated. A cultural system is different from a social system in the sense that it is more expansive. A cultural system includes four elements: knowledge, techniques, beliefs and space.

The four major components of a cultural system

Knowledge

First and foremost, a culture is a learning patrimony, that is to say, a knowing of the world, a 'science'. Along with Western science, which considers itself 'universal', there are 'sciences' within all other civilizations, all exotic ethnic groups. These are called ethnosciences. They are *sciences outside the Western world*, be they sciences as such or pre-modern knowledge. In our postmodern world, in which ideas of progress and universal science seem somewhat less absolute than before, there is renewed interest in such pre-modern knowledge. For instance, Australian Aboriginal culture is highly regarded today whereas it was still viewed with contempt at the beginning of the 1950s.

Melanesians knew the arts of trepanning and massage, and had knowledge of the body that led to plant-based therapies, also

called ethnopharmaceutics. Melanesians were also well versed in
the art of gardening and were knowledgeable about soils; in brief
they had agronomic knowledge. Australian Aborigines are excel-
lent botanists and can recognize more than 200 plant species.
Today, this type of knowledge is invaluable. Many new medical
drugs entail isolating the molecules of plants used by so-called
'primitive' societies, whose rich cultural knowledge was unnoted
until now. For example, malaria was partly eradicated thanks to
quinine, an extract from a bitter tree bark which people in tropical
forests knew how to use therapeutically.[1]

In the Middle Ages, craftsmen had invented a shade of blue that
we no longer know how to reproduce. The Chinese elaborated acu-
puncture and remain the specialists of that technique. Pacific
Islanders mastered the art of navigation and can find their way
without a compass. They built canoes and crossed the entire Pacific
Ocean at a time when the islands in the Mediterranean Sea had not
even been settled. Traditional populations have techniques, types
of magic and shamanic practices that are linked with profound
forms of human knowledge. No one has to believe in these magical
practices, yet they evoke another side to human beings and their
psyche. Indeed, they are efficient in so far as they are based on the
human psyche. All ethnosciences, magic-based sciences and shamanic practices play a major role in the understanding of cultures.

A technical patrimony

Pre-modern forms of knowledge are linked with various techniques and tools. These may include building methods (houses,
churches, tombs), production methods, modes of production
(agrarian systems, fallow types, the shape of fields, plants under
cultivation, agrarian combinations, gathering techniques, ethno-
medicine, gastronomy),[2] the arts of hunting or fishing, and so
forth. All these techniques that are induced from traditional
knowledge are the signs of a culture, its markers; their spatial distribution is specific, and they delineate culture areas. A culture

avails itself of a technical heritage, which is an art connected with a 'geography', that is, a specific distribution area. Thus, tile and slate roof types in France outline two culture areas: 'France d'oc' and 'France d'oïl'.[3]

We speak of rice, wine, yam, or wheat civilizations, since an agrarian system is not only the most efficient production technique within a specific environment but also a representation of the world, i.e. a culture.

The *genres de vie* or lifeways – Vidal de la Blache's key concept – rely on these basic techniques, which are themselves linked with a unique cultural purpose. Thanks to technology, human beings meet life's basic needs, or rather survival needs. There is nothing more cultural than the ways in which human beings endeavour to survive, for the methods they use always go beyond the sheer satisfaction of surviving *stricto sensu*. This is perhaps what differentiates humans from animals. The concept of *genre de vie* corresponds to elementary survival techniques and constitutes one of the basic elements of culture.

Beliefs

Customarily referred to as the upper level of culture, knowledge and techniques 'outside the Western world' are based on beliefs, religions and specific worldviews. This upper echelon also represents the very foundation of culture – its roots, i.e. that which holds the whole. Within it, there is always a basic link between values and techniques, between what looks toward the sky and what is 'down-to-earth'. What makes cultural geography interesting is the fact that all societies draw their essential understanding from the worldview that they adopt, in other words, from their representations. A worldview is expressed through founding myths, either traditional or modern, and a symbolic discourse.

This discourse reveals the basic values that permeate society and collective mentalities.

- Cultures represent more than a *genre de vie*, i.e. a way to live or to survive; they are also an art of living and even a reason to live. A culture gives sense and meaning to the world; it offers a vision of the world and organizes thought processes.
- This ordering of thought processes is based on a belief system as well as myths and values. In turn, these elements give rise to specific forms of ethics, aesthetics, morals and art. Any human group builds itself through a cultural order at once ethical and aesthetic – both are linked. This cultural order rests on reason and sensibility. Cultures need to believe in themselves; otherwise chaos ensues.
- The cultural worldview explains the world; it is a way to see, perceive and sense it. In other words, it is a representation. Any culture is a system of representation. The French do not have the same representations of the world, the cosmos, life and death as the Japanese, nor even as culturally closer neighbours like the Americans. The Africans of the savanna and the Africans of the Sahel region do not have the same representation of trees as forest-based Africans. They do not have the same representations or the same tastes food-wise, or the same view of bush fires or religion. The forest is always a world of spirits: while it is an enchanted space in the eyes of those who live there, others fear it. Polynesian and Melanesian representations of the sea are different.

Representations find their expression in acts and discourses but mostly through mythology, *founding myths* in particular. These narratives, more or less magnified, delineate a culture's basic values, which are the values acknowledged by the major part of a society. Founding myths are essential to our understanding of traditional societies. In this respect we must read Mircea Eliade, who speaks of civilizing heroes that have shaped the Melanesian world and played the role of cultural models: Tagaro, Mwatiktiki, Maui and the like.

Founding myths underlie tradition – and the modernity that aims at replacing tradition. In traditional cultures, the golden age often lies in the past and is situated at the origin. In modern cultures, the golden age is the myth of progress and therefore lies in the future. For instance, the myth inspired by Jean-Jacques Rousseau in the eighteenth century is situated at the opposite of the traditional myth. According to this philosopher, civilization, and therefore culture, corrupts humankind, which is naturally endowed with the right instincts. Hence comes the idea of a social contract to preserve human beings from an unjust society; and hence the dream of a cultural liberation. This example involves a mythology of its own, one that is still pivotal today. Myths and worldviews are expressed through symbols such as the Christian cross, the *fleur-de-lis* of French royalty, the hammer-and-sickle, flags, etc.

Territories are powerful markers within which symbols become visible. These spatial symbols, or geosymbols, include symbolic places that are at once significative and meaningful, e.g. the forests of ancient druids; Mont Saint-Michel in western France; the Bastille, Champs-Elysées, and Sorbonne in Paris. These are identity-bearing geosymbols. Indeed, no identity exists without a space that sustains it, or without a territory marked by geosymbols.

A geosymbol is 'the imprint within a place of an inscribing process focused on memory. May be considered as geosymbol any place, site, space, itinerary, natural feature, spring, or human construction that gives meaning to landscape and thereby expresses and nurtures the identity of populations or ethnic groups.' (Bonnemaison 1992)

Representations, worldviews, myths and geosymbols give strength to belief systems. They underlie all cultures. They structure and sustain the order of the mind; in other words, they keep culture alive.

Major cultures are identified with major religions. Belief is always steeped in memory, itself transmuted to myth. Without memory of the past there can be no culture or future. The further in time the mining of memory, the richer the culture. The absence of references to the past, or a cultural life that is linked only with the present, or the attitude of 'living in the moment', in the fashion of the times, with its mannerisms, are all drift-like modern symptoms. They lead us to turn our backs to genuine profoundness and authentic culture; only artificial and superficial aspects matter, negating culture.

In some cases, ideology may replace religious belief. Ideology manifests itself through a seemingly rational discourse but also through hidden myths. Like religions, it builds itself up from a foundation of faith. Marxism, for example, the religion of man without God, intends to open up 'joyful tomorrows' on earth thanks to the struggle of the toiling classes, akin to a sort of redeeming Christianity. The same can be said of the myth of the global market – a creed shared by all bankers and supporters of metaphysical liberalism – and also of nationalism and, when it existed, fascism. From ideology to belief there is but one step, which is often taken too rapidly.

Thus a worldview is a system made of four elements: representations, founding myths, geosymbols and a memory. This system represents the upper level of culture. Cultures are like human lives: they can fade away and die. Yet mentalities and cultures are often resilient as they continue to leap from one era to the next. Their transformation is very gradual, however. They resist; sometimes they become weak.

Ideology can play the same role. Flowing from a discourse or a myth, ideology constructs itself as a rational system, albeit on foundations that are actually dependent on belief.

A space

Cultures organize themselves spatially. Whatever their size, cultures are always localized. Historian Fernand Braudel said that cultures have a geographical dwelling. Cultures are united to a geographical environment, they respond to it, but they cannot be explained by it (i.e. there is no such thing as environmental determinism). On the contrary, there is a continuous dialectic between geographical setting and culture – a sort of dialogue and also a struggle. The human environment and the natural environment can never be separated; one does not explain the other, none has meaning by itself; their reciprocal relation creates geographical milieu and cultural milieu. In short, cultural geography also deals with space, land, topography, climate, vegetation, animal species as well as natural assets and constraints.[4]

For instance, there are two major Indian cultures: 'humid' India with heavy rainfall, lakes, swamps, aquatic vegetation, jungles and dark-skinned people; 'dry' India, centred on the Middle Indus and the Ganges, with light-skinned people who have often been conquering warriors. There is a connection between the two types of humanity, the two milieux; India is the result of a 'dialogue' (and, at times, a struggle) between these two cultures.

Another example is that of Melanesians and Polynesians. Melanesians have settled in large islands; they are land-based rather than shore-based, they are men of one place[5] who have built egalitarian societies without great leaders. Polynesians live on lower, smaller islands. They are fishermen, people of the sea who have built kingdoms. Polynesian society is war-prone and hierarchical, with kings and priests.

There are cultures of the sea, cultures of the river (the role of great rivers in the construction of cultural identity is essential, e.g. the Nile, Euphrates, Ganges, Yellow River, Danube …), mountain, delta, or forest cultures, and so forth. A geographer should never neglect the force of the natural setting. The natural setting always

challenges a society to surpass itself; society's response to environmental challenges creates culture. The greater the challenge, the
more determining the response.

Network society and reticulated space: the case of Vanuatu

An island always represents a rupture, an end to the road, a
shore of anxiety [...]. Once on land, once the ship or canoe
has left, one's link to the great movement of time is severed
[...]. What remains is space. Narrow, closed, and bordered
by the endless motion of waves, that space is rare and therefore infinitely precious. It becomes the one and only value.

The navigating people that discovered the islands of Vanuatu by canoe turned their discovery into a 'place-based
culture'. Out of these splintered lands, which seemed devoid
of linkages and outside time, they carved their own truth;
within these closed horizons they rooted their destiny; from
the places where they landed and from their first island walks
they fashioned signs of foundation, which then became the
first marks of their identity [...]. Melanesian Islanders do not
look at the sky but at the earth [...]. They are trees, trees
with deep roots that dig earthward, toward the magical foundations of the world [...].

Melanesian places are not of width but of depth [...]. Just
as the landscape is scattered with trees, space is strewn with
men ples 'men of one place'[6] [...]. Places shape men; roads are
what makes places. Keeping the memory of their origin,
islanders focus on travels and roads as much as on places and
roots. Melanesian metaphors express this original duality.
Man is a tree while the local group is a canoe [...]. From each
place roads originate in star-like patterns that outline collective paths. Although a man is expected to remain within his
places, he must also explore the roads set by his canoe. These

roads allow for outside alliances and, often, marriage alliances as well [...].

The *man-tree*[7] can only live through the *group-canoe* that gives him the allies necessary for his survival and reproduction. Each territory of custom represents a fragment of road, a nexus of places, a system of trees and canoes [...]. Thus, societies in the Vanuatu archipelago are network-based and set in an open-ended relational space. Through culture, society has attempted to give itself the linkages that nature did not offer [...]. Within traditional Melanesian society space is not perceived through its divisions or its limits but through road-based relations [...]. There are no central places in this type of space [...]. It is an axiom of custom that each place along the road is equal to the others. Indeed, in order for the relation to continue, the presence of each road segment is indispensable. Should one link collapse or should one of the places die, the road then breaks down [...]. Melanesian roads converge toward crossroads, but they also trace back to founding places, which are the places of their emergence [...].

A *founding place* differs from a *central place*. The latter makes the rest of the structure converge toward itself. The former pushes out the forces that rise up within its core; instead of creating a periphery, it recreates similar places, which carry its power or a fragment of it farther away, in chain-like fashion [....]. The destiny of the Melanesian canoe is to expand its relation of alliance to the farthest limits indicated by the roads within its territory. This horizon does not loop back onto itself; it projects a link that is literally infinite.

J. Bonnemaison, *Gens de pirogue et gens de la terre. Les fondements géographiques d'une identité: l'archipel du Vanuatu* (revised edition of *L'Arbre et la pirogue*), Paris, ORSTOM, 1996, 433–6.

Space also plays the role of buttress. The spatial distribution of cultures creates culture areas (cf. Frobenius 1952). This theme is highly geographical; indeed, it stands at the core of cultural geography. A *culture area* may be defined as a relatively homogeneous space, within which prevails the dominant association of specific cultural traits. In traditional societies, this association may involve a language, a type of ritual, hunting weapons, pottery, or a weaving technique.

At another scale, civilizations fashion more complex culture areas, which can be broken down into specific areas. Such is the case of the Western, Islamic, African, Far Eastern civilizations as well as Oceania and others. Civilizations are characterized by a dominant combination of cultural traits and by shared paradigms.

But these culture areas are not closed off, they send and receive; they exchange cultural traits. They are born from an intense circulation, which they help perpetuate. Cultures have been communicating on a permanent basis since antiquity or prehistoric times. In the Pacific, obsidian arrowheads and jade ornaments were being exchanged over thousands of miles – by canoe, from one island to another – 5,000 years ago.

The example of *kava* illustrates three levels that together help shape a cultural system: culture area, space-as-experienced and cultural space.

This plant, *Piper methysticum,* only grows in Oceania. It is cultivated, prepared and marketed in the region. Numerous varieties are known and have been developed through speciation (i.e. one can get new species from a single stock). A geographer will find it interesting to examine, through space and time, the diffusion area of *kava*, a cultural plant par excellence.

Through the ritual preparation of this plant one obtains a social and sacred beverage. Taking the variety of species into account, cultivation techniques as well as preparation and consumption methods follow a number of island customs. Thus the plant can be chewed, grated, cut, or ground into a powder. When Tanna Islanders drink *kava*, the ambiance is convivial; each participant prepares the beverage for a friend; the youngest men prepare it for the elders. Only men may participate in the ritual. At nightfall, the leader begins the ceremony by drinking *kava*, then it is the turn of the guest of honour and *small men*[8] in order to abide by a certain hierarchical order. The leader then shouts to invoke ancestors. As the effects of *kava* become stronger, silence progressively seizes the crowd until all become quiet in *tamafa*, absolute silence.

The social practice of *kava* drinking has evolved. The ritual used to be reserved to leaders on great occasions; rarely did *small men* partake of it. Today the practice is more widespread than before. Men drink it daily in some cases and prepare it so as to make its taste more pleasant. Thus *kava* is now a beverage; it is no longer a ritual. In addition, under the influence of Europeans, the practice is becoming marginal and *kava* is simply seen as a drug.[9]

Kava also represents an iconography, in the sense given to it by Jean Gottmann.

Kava refers to a cultural space and expresses a vision of the world (cf. 'The *nakamal* in Vanuatu'). Thanks to the dreams it helps generate, *kava* drinking facilitates the dialogue with ancestors. Melanesians 'listen to the song of *kava*'; their spirit leaves their body and thus they can be close to their ancestors.

A woman is at the source of the *kava* myth, which is the reason why women are excluded from the ritual. Because she was too inconstant, this original woman was killed. A plant eventually germinated from her body and grew through the soil above her. Rats came to eat the roots, became euphoric, and went to sleep. Men then tasted the roots and decided that *kava* would be suitable as a beverage for leaders.

The *nakamal* (men's house) in Vanuatu

[In Vanuatu,] traditional settlements consist of small hamlets, generally comprised of less than a dozen houses. These hamlets used to be enclosed by a fence [...]. A hamlet corresponds to an extended family or an exogamous lineage segment [...]. Hamlets are distant from each other by a few hundred or dozen metres, thereby creating a common area for residential and convivial purposes; together, they make up what may be called a local residential group [...]. A local group has a political reality, which is made tangible by the presence of a men's house (or *nakamal*) [...]. While the household space of women is enclosed and was, in the past, surrounded by a fence, the social space of men is open [...]. It is the place par excellence for social meetings. The presence of women is strictly prohibited, especially in the evenings when the men are together [...].

Throughout the archipelago, men from the local group, along with their allies who are visiting, gather together at nightfall. In many islands, this is the time when men prepare the *kava* ceremonial for each other. *Kava* is extracted from the roots of a wild pepper plant, which the men chew or grind and then mix with running water; the beverage has narcotic properties [...]. Rather than drinking as such, being together and talking are the highlights of the daily *nakamal* meeting. The *nakamal* is a social and political place as well as the centre of the local group and the very symbol of its presence as an autonomous local community. There are as many types of *nakamal* as there are culture areas. In the northern part of the archipelago the *nakamal* is a long house that can hold thirty or forty men; from a distance, its roof looks like a conch. Central pillars uphold the internal structure and compartmentalize it [...]. Together, men eat their evening meal near fires whose embers glow continuously.

Even though the *nakamal* is a communal space, it is always linked with the ranked man who initiated its construction. The *nakamal*'s organization is a symbolic reflection of the group's inner hierarchy [...]. Common men are assigned to the fires near the entrance. Away from the entrance there is a progressive sequence of compartments and fires near which only high-ranking men are allowed to stay. In the back of the *nakamal*, space becomes sacred. [...] All the treasured possessions of the group are – or were – deposited in these sacred houses, whose size and beauty are proportional to the prestige and quality of the rank held by the big man who holds the dominating position [...]. When a *nakamal* is completed, the opening ritual involves all those who have a relation of alliance with the local group. All come to dance [...] and give away mats and pigs; they receive equivalent gifts in return [...].

The traditional landscape is thus without villages or apparent order. It is made up of women's household places as well as social places for convivial gatherings where men establish political relationships. A local group is characterized by the various family hamlets that are linked to the political *nakamal* houses. Similarly, the pattern of *nakamal* houses defines the structure of local groups and that of the region.

J. Bonnemaison, *Gens de pirogue et gens de la terre. Les fondements géographiques d'une identité: l'archipel du Vanuatu* (revised edition of *L'Arbre et la pirogue*), Paris, ORSTOM, 1996, 199–205.

A universal mission

Today, the diffusion of goods and cultural traits is considerably faster. Cultures collide with the supremacy of one culture among them, which is perceived as the model of the future. By proclaiming its universality, Western civilization elevates itself to the status of dominant model for the so-called 'traditional' societies. Western civilization is seen as 'modern'. It holds the keys to progress, which merges with its own triumph. This situation is the first of its kind in the history of the world, whereby human beings confront each other less in physical terms than in cultural terms. Cultural power is more important than other forms of power. It is the root of political power: the issue is to take hold of minds, the rest will follow (cf. Gramsci). Once there was a clash of nations; we are now moving towards a *clash of civilizations* involving enormous cultural stakes.

Knowledge, *techniques*, *belief* and *space* are the four pillars of a cultural system. Each culture has its own way of combining these factors and each ethnic group has its own culture. The ethnogeographic approach[10] deals with the geography of a given culture, just as ethnology is the study of a given ethnic group.

The term of ethnogeography carries another connotation. It investigates the representation of space in a given cultural system, including the role of land tenure, the type of relationship with the land, wayfinding methods, practices to represent the geographic milieu, and finally the role of space in the construction of cultural identity. The territory plays an essential role in this respect. Cultural identity is *the marrying of an ethnic group and a territory*. Rather than an actual entity, the territory may be conjured up. Such is the case of diasporas (e.g. Israel and the Promised Land).

The organization of a cultural system's elements

Since cultural geography is a fairly new discipline, it is important to define its terminology. As mentioned earlier, a cultural system may be defined through the four major themes of knowledge, techniques, belief and space. It can also be defined through its internal organization, whereby material and spiritual elements become integrated at various levels and scales, from the local to the global.

Cultural geographers make a distinction between four levels, from the simplest to the most complex: cultural traits or cultural elements, cultural ensembles or complexes, cultures, and civilizations. The level of aggregation varies from small to large, not unlike a Russian *matrushka* doll. The smallest elements cluster within a higher-level element. Thus a civilization gathers several cultures, which themselves include cultural ensembles defined in turn by a plurality of cultural traits.

Cultural traits or cultural elements

An element is the constituent part of an object that, when combined with various other elements, makes up another object. We speak of the 'elements of a problem', elements of knowledge and natural elements. In mathematics, the element is one of the items that make up an ensemble. The four elements – water, earth, air and fire – used to be considered as the constituent ingredients of all substances. From a chemical standpoint, an element is a simple body. Culturally speaking, an element represents a trait, a component of an ensemble. It is the simplest cultural element that can be discerned, be it material, spiritual, or artistic. Examples follow, in no particular order:

- A piece of pottery, such as Lapita pottery in the South Pacific;
- A flint implement;
- A feathered arrow;
- A dance, chant, or poem;
- A tool, such as a plough or a telephone;
- A type of clothing: a sandal, a penis sheath, or a grass skirt;
- A simple ritual element – social or religious;
- A way to greet, kiss, or touch (or not touch) others;
- An element of the cultural landscape, such as a hedge, a stone path, a village. A landscape is made out of a combination of elements. The first step is to identify them.

Cultural ensemble (cultural complex or cultural cycle)

A cultural ensemble bundles together various cultural traits that are set toward the same purposes.

For example, to milk a cow, drink milk, churn butter, eat it, make yogurts and cheese, and so forth, are all cultural traits that are connected within the 'milk cultural complex' of a cattle-raising community.

Similarly, to raise oxen, to yoke them to a plough or to a cart, to tan hides and turn these into shoes and clothing, all these activities partake of a cultural ensemble that can be qualified as an 'ox complex'. It is linked with the milk cultural ensemble but may also be distinguished from it.

An example of archaeological cultural ensemble is Lapita pottery, which combines all elements linked with pottery such as chisel, bracelets and food.

Other cultural ensembles may be given as examples:
• A language;
• A complex ritual cycle with plural meanings that integrates several rhythmic or sung components, gifts and counter-gifts, symbols, etc., e.g. the *toka* ritual in the island of Tanna, with its cycle of dances, songs, costumes, gift-giving, pigs and ornaments;
• A set of behaviours;
• A landscape; a wood/forest/field grouping or a *terroir*;[11]
• A set of clothes;
• A type of equipment, i.e. a set of tools;
• A corpus of texts or oral literature;
• A great myth with multiple episodes.

An ensemble can include sub-components.

To study a culture one needs to split it into ensembles, possibly into sub-ensembles and elements, and then analyse this combination of factors.

Culture

Culture blends various cultural complexes within a global *cultural system*.

The Lapita complex blends with the Lapita culture, which includes a language, an environment, networks, etc.

The milk cultural complex and the ox-breeding complex both belong to the same system, that of cattle breeders, which can be found with differing variations over a wide diversity of geographic spaces.

A culture, i.e. a cultural system, includes several ensembles. Lapland culture combines the milk cultural complex with reindeer harnessing and training, clothes made of reindeer hides, myths and legends connected with reindeer, geographic routes followed by herds, and so forth – a series of ensembles that blend with each other.

Here is a more familiar example. Let us assume that we are carrying out a geocultural survey of the Department of Geography at the University Paris IV Sorbonne:

- A course represents a cultural trait;
- A degree is a cultural ensemble or a cultural cycle;
- A department (UFR) is a cultural system with its body of knowledge, teaching and management techniques, founding myths, beliefs, 'heroes', space, traditions – in short, this cultural system characterizes the department's identity.

Civilization

Cultures are part of a civilization; they blend with the upper level of civilizations. It is a question of scale. Indeed some cultural traits and complexes may belong to several cultures or civilizations. For instance, the sport of rugby is a cultural complex in itself, a culture, that also refers to several national cultures.[12]

Another example is that of the *nekowiar* in Melanesia, a ritual cycle of alliance between political groups in the course of which dances, pigs and food are exchanged:

- The *toka* dance represents a cultural trait (thirty dancers).
- The *toka* ritual (2,000 participants) is part of this cultural complex (with songs, gifts, counter-gifts, pig sacrifice, etc.) and can only be understood within a system.
- The ritual merges into the cultural system of Tanna (20,000 inhabitants), along with other complexes such as pig husbandry, yam culture, mythical cycles, *kava*, and so forth. Other islands may share some of these complexes.
- Along with other cultures, Tanna's island culture belongs to Melanesian culture (which concerns two to three million inhabitants).
- In turn, Melanesian culture merges with the civilization of Oceania (currently accounting for six or seven million inhabitants).

We can also speak of a reindeer culture. This trans-territorial culture unites a wide group of Arctic, Amerindian and Siberian communities. Another example is that of the ox culture, which is not only spread over various spaces but connects sharply different cultures and cultural systems. Some geographers have investigated the concept of a chestnut-tree culture (Pitte 1986).

At a higher, trans-geographic level, one may speak of these cultures as civilizations. For instance, Pierre Gourou described a rice civilization. To go back to the UFR example, there is, beyond the Parisian university culture, a civilization of scientific knowledge represented by the various universities worldwide.

The elements that make up the cultural approach parallel the mosaic of spatial scales. Each element of the approach corresponds to a spatial level. This is, of course, the province of geography.

The spaces of culture

When a specific culture and a territory are linked, we speak of cultural space. Similar connections can occur between various levels of the cultural construction and various spatial components. Thus we distinguish cultural places and hearths, regions, culture areas and finally cultural worlds.

Cultural hearth

Here is the heart of a culture, its 'capital city', and frequently its place of origin. As a rule, a cultural element is linked with a hearth and a diffusion area. A hearth is a territory where ideas and cultural practices were conjured up and constructed, and from which they have spread through spatial differentiation. A hearth may exist at one of several scales, either as a locality or a region. The hearth is the birthplace of origin. For France, it is the Île-de-France region.[13] The hearth of Lapita culture is the northern part of Papua New Guinea (PNG). The East Asian hearth is Northern China, where agricultural techniques (millet and kaoliang[14] as dry cultures vs. irrigated rice cultivation in South China), together with a culture and a civilization, developed from cultural traits and complexes that were simple at the outset, then spread while they differentiated throughout the Chinese mainland, its peninsulas – Vietnam and Korea – and its archipelago – Japan. In this respect we may speak of a core. There a civilization began, drawing from several cultural systems whose common origin is precisely situated in space.

Each culture, each great civilization has its own cultural hearth(s). Mesopotamia, the Nile Valley, the Indus Basin, the plains of the Ganges and Huang He (Yellow River), Greece and the Aegean Islands are the cultural birthplaces of the world's major civilizations.

Other examples abound. The heart of Quebec is Quebec City and the plain of Lac St Jean near the mouth of the St Lawrence River. The heart of the French university system is the Sorbonne, owing as much to its origin as to its prestige. French geography was born at the Institute of Geography. *And you are here.*[15] The Institute has a soul.

The milk culture has several hearths: Bulgaria for yogurt and the northwestern fringe of Europe as the birthplace of cheeses and cheese making.

Ideologies and the world of the sacred as well as more earthly cultural complexes all have a hearth or cultural centre in the guise of a point (or channel) of origin and a diffusion area. The heart of Christianity is Jerusalem, with the Holy Sepulchre; that of Islam, Mecca. For a long time the core of Marxism was Moscow; today it is Cuba.

The cultural region or 'pays' (a cultural complex and its area of expansion)

When the reach of a cultural complex corresponds to a precise geographic space, a cultural region is created. For example, Korea and Japan form cultural regions. These two countries share a number of cultural traits and ensembles, which are combined into their own cultural systems. In North America Quebec makes up a homogeneous cultural region united through its language and memory (cf. the motto on car plates: '*Je me souviens*', 'I remember'). Anglo-Canada is another. Perhaps there are two countries: French Canada and Anglo-Canada, the eastern provinces and the western provinces. The United States forms another region (or several, as the case may be). So does Mexico.

The scale of a cultural region can vary. The island of Tanna in Vanuatu makes up a cultural region by itself to the extent that its culture is unique and different from others; it is based on the complex of the *toka* ritual. Quebec relies on the francophone complex. Lapland's cultural region is linked with the reindeer complex. Both the Bara shepherds in Madagascar and the Masai in Kenya and Tanzania belong to the ox complex.

From a certain point of view, the cheese-producing regions in France form a cultural region that can be divided into regional sub-complexes or *pays*. The *pays* correspond to the various types of cheese that are made within a particular milk complex. The same type of linkage applies to wine production.

Thus each cultural region may be subdivided into sub-regions according to a specific set of criteria.

Culture areas (a culture and its space)

A culture area gathers a set of cultural regions joined by common paradigms or an identical cultural foundation. Thus, the cultural regions of North America – Quebec, Anglo-Canada in the eastern and western provinces, and the United States – form a culture area in so far as they correspond to a common North American culture. Mexico belongs to this geographical ensemble – which, thanks to NAFTA, has recently become an economic ensemble as well. However, Mexico parts from it from a cultural standpoint since it belongs to Latin America in that respect; it does so without making an issue of it and without soul searching.

This is not the case of Quebec. The ambiguity of Quebec stems from the fact that, as a cultural region, it is part of the North American culture area and shares many of its traits through its way of life. Yet Quebec is also outside America by reason of its language and affective links with France and the culture area of Northwestern Europe. Hence ambivalence and heartbreak, along with the temptation of either Canadian federalism or separatism (Canadians themselves speak of 'sovereignty'). As a cultural region, Quebec is torn between two culture areas.

For its part, Northwestern Europe represents a culture area that includes several regions joined by common cultural traits and ensembles. It is different from Mediterranean Europe and Central

Europe, which are themselves connected with different cultures. Similarly, the geographical spread of Melanesian culture at the heart of the Pacific forms a culture area within which co-exist several original regions.[16] China, Japan, Korea and Vietnam form a culture area, that of East Asia, whose hearth is Northern China. The Maghreb (North Africa) is also a culture area.

For a culture area to exist there must be a large enough space and a measure of spatial continuity.

Cultural worlds (civilization and space)

The metacultural dimension

We now investigate a final type of space, a final component of the cultural system, perhaps the most fundamental. Beyond civilizations and great cultures, there is an ultimate level: the metacultural. What is *metaculture*?

The root *meta* expresses the idea that there is a hidden aspect beyond the word itself, with a still deeper connotation. *Meta* addresses that which lies beyond, that which incorporates. Here are a few examples. As a fundamental part of philosophy, *metaphysics* deals with beingness, seen as a totality, and searches for an explanation of it beyond the world perceived by the senses. *Metamorphosis* is a change of form, so considerable and complete that the being or object is no longer recognizable. The initial form has been totally transformed into a form beyond itself. A *metamessage* is a message about messages, a *metasystem* a system about systems. *Metapolitics* is that which, beyond politics, controls politics. It is a grand vision, either a vision of the world or a vision of humanity. There is no true politics without a metapolitical vision beyond it that easily transcends the usual political rifts, such as the left/right or reformist/conservative binomials. Great men and women are characterized by their ability to stand at that level. As to *metaphor*, it implies that, beyond the image, there is another meaning, which is accessible through a transferring process. One uses a figurative term to represent a more abstract reality: instead of the 'cause' of the problem one may speak of the 'root' of the problem; the 'origin' of the affliction is the 'source' of the affliction. Many communities speak through the agency of images, for these deliver profound meanings beyond representation.

Meta signifies the fundamental crux, that which is beyond, that which touches on the very essence of things. In terms of research, *meta* represents the ultimate questioning.

Hence one can speak of metaculture to designate a domain beyond cultures, which is therefore part of civilization's reach. Beyond cultural differences, there are more fundamental cultural links that unite humans and societies, in other words, cultural levels that are more inclusive than others.

To the level of metaculture corresponds a fundamental spatial level. That is the level of 'cultural worlds'. In this case, *world* takes on two meanings: that of 'cultural roots' and that of 'cultural basins', again speaking metaphorically. Some cultural worlds are best understood in network-like fashion and others through propinquity, i.e. through basins, through their positioning within the same stratum.

Cultural roots

A cultural world can be united in so far as it has a common basis or presents a universal message. Network-shaped cultural worlds include different cultures and civilizations; they express what is common to seemingly foreign cultures. This presupposes that, beyond these cultures and civilizations, there is a level that aims for universality. In the first analysis, such transverse cultural worlds correspond to great universal religions and major ideologies.

It all begins, of course, with great religions, which are metacultures that aim for the universal. Christianity, Islam, Buddhism, Hinduism have engendered cultural worlds that, beyond local cultures and regional spaces, weave a sort of network and encompass founding places, cultural hearths and common roots. Cultural and spatial roots give cohesiveness to these vast cultural worlds, which through them find their ultimate significance.

Also giving rise to cultural worlds are major ideologies, such as Marxism at its high point. With its emphasis on the market economy, today's humanistic liberalism lays the foundation of a cultural world as well.

Other movements are taking shape, heralding the birth of new cultural spaces. Modernity is a metaculture that transcends the notion of Western civilization, since it includes Japan and several newly industrialized countries in Asia. Post-modernity goes beyond modern civilization and outlines new patterns, whose boundaries are currently ill-defined yet real.

While cultural regions and areas assume a certain continuity or spatial proximity characterized by a homogeneous and continuous area, a cultural world may unite very distant spaces separated by geography; for instance, Islamic countries are steeped in one cultural world, and so are Catholic countries. These transverse cultural worlds are network-like spaces. They epitomize the world's current cultural and political pattern, a pattern that tends to be organized around major systems of alliance in network-like fashion rather than as blocs. The cohesiveness of these spaces is cultural first, geopolitical second.

In short, beyond regional cultures, there are metacultures, which are transverse to regions and nations. Metacultures are the foundation of civilizations. They correspond to cultural worlds that are organized according to two models:

- The first model is that of a network structure based on common cultural roots, such as the world's great religions, ideologies and major language families. One may speak of 'worlds' that refer to metacultures and therefore to common roots and to a hearth — the latter also being a heart, a spiritual centre, and in some cases a political core. The world is scattered with culture hearths, from which spatial networks derive. According to this model, the geocultural and geopolitical configuration of the contemporary world patterns itself along networks and major transterritorial systems of alliance.

- The second model is a structure built on geographical continuity, i.e. on propinquity or familiarity with the same environment. In this case one may speak of a 'cultural world' in the sense of cultural basin or common geographical matrix.

Cultural basins

New worlds may appear through a relation based on spatial proximity rather than through a common culture. A movement tends to unite or intensify communication between countries whose cultural roots are separate but which are geographically close. Such worlds have appeared and disappeared in the course of history. Today, geopolitical configurations worldwide are playing themselves out around cultural basins.

Mediterranean civilization is a case in point. In antiquity, the Mediterranean Sea was an inland lake, a communication channel, and an exchange platform that joined the fates of various populations and ethnic groups. Cultures and civilizations were part of the same world, at once geographical and cultural, while keeping their specificity. Far from setting communities apart, the sea allowed them to communicate: syncretisms, new systems and new religions were springing up. The Mediterranean Basin, which is a precise term in physical geography, was also a cultural basin, a very specific and well-defined geocultural world.

The unity of the Mediterranean world was forged before the Roman apotheosis when, on the basin's circumference, seafaring peoples reigned and prevailed over inland communities. A transverse culture then came into being thanks to the great thalassocracies[17] of Tyre, Crete, Athens and Carthage – all naval and trade-oriented powers.

At the dawn of Western history, the Mediterranean was a distinct world, the locus of a successful process of cultural cross-breeding. It became a cradle, a cultural compost that was particularly rich and out of which other civilizations sprang.

Yet nothing ever stays the same. The unity of the Mediterranean world broke down when the thalassocracies were eventually defeated by inland nations that were more warlike and more focused on conquest than trade. Once they had taken over the thalassocracies' legacy, they turned away from the shore and went back to their original reality – land. The cultural world of the Mediterranean split up once again and shattered into multiple fragments, into different cultures and civilizations: in particular the North broke away from the South. There still remains a memory of that initial grace period – the feeling of lost unity, nostalgia about an earlier cultural world.

Can the Mediterranean Basin be reborn as a cultural world? That is the issue. Such a renaissance would be likely to facilitate the emergence of a new geopolitical world, yet a number of political and cultural forces are now clashing within the region. The Mediterranean world can come back to life, but recent events suggest the opposite.

The new great cultural spaces

Today the world tends to be more unified as vast regions come into being. Joint organizations are being built on a political and economic basis – at least on the surface. Although hidden and rarely put forward, the cultural dimension is nevertheless essential. Indeed it may be the secret purpose of great alliances. Alliances are strong when they rely on major cultural networks or cultural basins. Obvious benefits are not sufficient; they are often secondary to affectivity, imagination and vision, which together represent the foundation of culture.

What has been called the Atlantic world corresponds to a political and cultural union. Europe is currently emerging as a geocultural and geopolitical union. As for the Pacific world, it appears to be primarily an economic union with some political dimensions and no cultural dimensions.

Today, major geocultural spaces are being delineated: Europe (European Union), North American (NAFTA) and APEC, which gathers eighteen states situated in the Pacific Ocean and along its rim. At this stage APEC is only an economic club that aims at developing internal trade, but it accounts for two billion inhabitants, i.e. 38 per cent of the world's population and over half of its gross national product. It includes three giants: the United States, China and Japan.

The Pacific Basin community may be seen as the emerging second axis of the world. Yet in order to succeed, that community must achieve cultural unity. It must find the inner links that will allow it to communicate: first, through business people and trade networks and also, and primarily, through a joint dialogue involving common representations and visions. Rudyard Kipling said, *'East is East, and West is West, and never the twain shall meet'*.[18] Should the Pacific Basin become a reality, the assumption is that East and West will meet; or at least they will pursue a dialogue about what they have in common and therefore become a cultural world, just as the Mediterranean Basin united its northern and southern rims in the past.

The Pacific community is only a potential community. It can transform itself, go beyond what it is today, or come to nothing and be shattered. The fate of the world, or at least that part of the world, depends on it.

Should a real cultural world emerge within the Pacific Basin, along with a political community, the Pacific would be likely to take power. It would become what the North Atlantic was for an entire century: the 'inland lake of the West', the founding crucible of the industrial revolution and democratic ideals, a basin rich in ideas and creations. After all, the military organization that unites the West carries the significant name of North Atlantic Treaty Organization, or NATO.

The concept of cultural world or basin underlies the birth and death of dominant geopolitical spaces. It represents the most inclusive level in the constructions of cultural geography. To the idea of civilization corresponds that of world. To the idea of metaculture corresponds that of a metaworld to come, with new cultural worlds and major axes where tomorrow's cultures and their political configurations are being created. That is the ultimate stage of cultural analysis. The world's major structuring processes are founded as much on joint values as on economic facts, on mind connections and divergences as much as on those of production. One and the other are indomitably linked.

Hence the idea that the world self-organizes in an interdependent mode along the lines of metacultures and metaworlds rather than national blocs.

Culture as process

A process is the evolution of a group of objects from a founding parameter. It is a dynamic that is self-regulating by means of an established rate of change and a sequence of chain reactions that push it forward. For example, industrialization, urbanization and acculturation are processes. Any culture is a process that can be broken down into five segments:

Discovery means that one finds a thing that already existed within the natural environment but whose usage was heretofore unknown, e.g. fire, coal, iron, viruses, medicinal or food plants (wheat, rice, tubers). One discovers a molecule or a new usage for a natural element. Discovery is not about creation but usefulness. Traditional cultures are often built on discoveries whose transforming effects are enormous.

Inventiveness creates something new, artificial, uniquely born of the human will, e.g. steel (an alloy that transforms iron) or television. It may be a ritual or a technique such as the printing process. Inventiveness drives the evolution of societies, especially when it gives rise to an innovation (Schumpeter 1911). Since we live in an increasingly artificial society (with its television-based culture),[19] discoveries are less plentiful than inventions.

Innovation is the application of an invention or a discovery to a technical domain or to daily life. For instance, the invention of the transistor led to a series of innovations in the electronics area. Sony's Walkman, created because the company founder, Akio Morita, wanted to play golf while listening to music, is an innovation based on the transistor. For cultural, socio-economic, or political reasons, some discoveries and inventions do not engender innovations. The fuel cell was originally invented over a century ago, yet it is only today that its use is being considered in the automobile industry.

Evolution is a movement that goes from simplicity to complexity, from the transformation of the initial innovation toward increasingly complex systems, e.g. automobiles and computer systems. Innovation never ceases; inventiveness evolves, calling for other inventions and transforming itself in the process. Progress ensues, as a rule, yet evolution can also turn into an endless race. As is commonly stated, 'progress cannot be stopped or mastered'. Some worry; and everyone feels powerless in the face of a number of evolutions. A few authors have spoken of mega-machinery; technology races ahead, no longer under human control.

Diffusion: As it evolves in time, a process spreads through space, e.g. the slow diffusion of the plough in Western Europe, the fast diffusion of the telephone, photocopy machine, fax machine, or recently the Internet. Wheat may also be seen as a cultural process. Originally from Asia, it was discovered, then reinvented through varietal selection and transformed through innovations and evolutions. Wheat slowly spread throughout the temperate world and its margins, eventually returning to Asia.

The English language is spreading worldwide, transforming itself into a quasi-universal language in the process: 'Basic English' is a simplified language which is increasingly different from the English spoken in England.

Thanks to the many foreign students in its universities and its powerful influence on international media, the United States spearheads a cultural model, that of the American way of life[20] whose values radiate throughout the world. As these values spread, they may turn into a 'Coca-Cola culture', however.

Colonization and military invasions have a cultural impact that includes the rapid diffusion of cultural models and goods, e.g. Rome and its colony of Gaul, or European colonial empires in the nineteenth and twentieth centuries.

The cultural process is an unceasing movement that brings about a series of chain reactions. It is likely to reverse itself or initiate feedback loops. Thus Gaul colonized Rome just as Rome recolonized its Germanic invaders. Any cultural process is interactive. Any diffusion is a complex process with feedback loops and multiple bifurcations that may change its significance.

The contemporary world has witnessed a prodigious acceleration of the phenomena of novelty diffusion. That may be the strongest characteristic of modernity. The Earth used to be a mosaic of cultural blocs that were tightly closed and ethnically homogeneous, like archipelagos or island blocs. Discoveries and inventions were accidental. Their diffusion was very slow, gradually crossing political boundaries or physical obstacles. They became known processes only when humans and societies progressively discovered their effects.

Diffusion varies according to the degree of openness of a society: the more open the society, the faster the diffusion.

Cultural mosaic

The more advanced a society, the more complex and heterogeneous its culture and the faster its innovation processes. Modern societies now have a formidable impact on the environment, an impact that was unthinkable in the past. This is a major concern of our times, for the planet's environment no longer internalizes the processes that affect it.

Two great revolutions have taken place in the history of humanity: the Neolithic agricultural revolution, whose diffusion processes were very slow, and the industrial revolution, whose diffusion processes have intensified and accelerated in the last 200 years. We are headed towards a third revolution – that of computer systems and communication – whose hallmark is rapidity.

The Earth has become a cultural mosaic characterized by the prodigiously swift diffusion of cultural processes. This diffusion is such that cultural processes tend to make the world uniform. I wish to emphasize the fact that they make it uniform, not united – for better and for worse. This intensification of cultural processes leads to a certain Westernization of the world, but it also involves backlash effects, bifurcations and emerging processes of rejection and reaction. The technical unification of the world represents a totally new situation in history. It produces two antagonistic forces: homogenization on the one hand and, on the other hand, a sort of political and cultural Balkanization, a withdrawal of many cultures as they turn down this universal model because of its Western overlay. The game is not over and the 'global village' may just be a delusion.

In brief, a dual movement that is entirely contradictory is taking place today. There is Westernization of the world into a basic culture, at once technical, aesthetic and ethical, along with a way of life and a way of thinking. Humanity discovers its universality in it. Simultaneously the world is becoming more commonplace, acculturated, and seemingly poorer in cultural terms. One part of the world dominates the rest, a situation which some authors, such as Régis Debray, expose in their writings.[21] This planetary space is an illusion, for there is neither exchange nor reciprocity, only the imposition of one viewpoint.

This same movement brings about a re-emergence of ethnic groups and territories as well as a renewal of the irrational and the sacred. Both effects herald the revolt of the local against the global. This debate currently divides intellectuals, governments and populations. It is not a dialogue but a strong-arm conflict, a relation of forces.

In terms of ideas there is now a controversy between modern and postmodern. I will conclude this chapter with two questions:

- Are there superior cultures, great cultures and sub-cultures?
- How does one explain cultural diversity if humankind is one entity? This question relates to cultural differences and their distribution on the surface of the earth. Therefore it involves geography.

These two major issues call for an entire university course as well as a type of knowledge and experience which only a few outstanding authors have mastered, without solving these problems completely. Here again there is an ongoing debate. I will only make a few remarks at this stage, for all disciplines in the human sciences attend to these issues.

Cultures and sub-cultures

Anthropology studies have emphasized the importance of collective identities. They have defined cultural groups such as ethnic, regional, or national groups. The characteristics of these cultures influence the behaviour of individuals who internalize values, principles and major ideas. This is what has been called cultural determinism or culturalism, considered as the primary factor that explains historical and sociological phenomena as well as the shaping of mentalities.

Some authors view culture as immanent wisdom that programmes individuals, informs them about their role and gives them an identity.

In the case of small, simple, egalitarian societies, notably hunter-gatherers or small peasant societies, culture, technology, faith and belief are common goods shared by all (Clastres 1974, 1980). Individuals are in full agreement with a tradition which they have internalized or a faith which they share; their cultural choices are those of their group. Tradition's authenticity is born from tradition's autochtony. Autochthony is the rooting of a people (and a cultural tradition) in a territory. That feeling may be quite strong, in which case a people identifies with both a culture and a territory – cf. the works of Béatrice Collignon on the Inuit, Sylvie Poirier (1996) on the Aborigines of Australia's Western Desert, and Philippe Descola (1993) on the Jivaro in the Amazonian rainforest.

In contrast, social differentiation within more complex agricultural or urban societies gives rise to dominant groups, i.e. a 'super-structure' of major owners, administrators, priests, judges and soldiers. The groups that manage live in town, the groups that are managed live in the country. In this case, a popular culture, a mass culture, differentiates itself from the culture of élites; society loses its cultural homogeneity.

Popular culture is occasionally equated to folklore. A non-élitist ideology holds that society's creativity and truth are found within popular culture: among peasants in the past, within urban masses today. Inversely, an élitist ideology holds that creativity and creators are found within the cultured élite: this is Xavier de Planhol's argument in his *Géographie historique de la France* (1988).

The culture of the élite is more open, more universal than popular culture, which is more localized and relies on oral communication. But movies and television have engendered a mass culture that is no longer tied to local roots.

The increasing complexity of society is shattering culture. Sub-cultures or counter-cultures appear as part of social or political stakes; struggles for cultural power tackle ideas, visions and values. At another scale, one may ask whether major cultures can be compared with minor cultures and whether hierarchies exist among cultures. That is the main question in the eyes of all researchers who investigate cultural factors.

Cultural differences

Cultures, be they present or past, are innumerable. We only know about one-tenth of them – the emerged part of the iceberg. According to Claude Lévi-Strauss, this diversity is structural; it is linked to the life of humanity and is part of its history. Diversity is a source of enrichment: it is a rainbow rather than a pyramid. But how can one interpret such diversity? With the clichés of evolutionism? We then have to deal with social or cultural Darwinism and, unavoidably, the approach of Walter W. Rostow (1962), economic advisor to President John F. Kennedy. According to Rostow's model, which is now outdated and even discredited, human history is divided into four stages:

- *Initial stage*: Nothing is happening, nothing moves; societies are immobile, without history; they are traditional or cold societies.[22]
- *Stage one*: Take-off. Society is now in transition; the beginning of the end of cultures is taking place.
- *Stage two*: Intermediary stage of evolution. The transitional society reaches a level of maturity considered as progress.
- *Final stage*: The ultimate stage, that of the consumer society. It is also the end of history, the apotheosis of the market economy and the American way of life,[23] i.e. mass culture and society.

According to this model, the primitive is archaic and the ultimate stage of humanity is the consumer society of Europe and North America. This viewpoint has come under much criticism; it illustrates the risk of proceeding from biological facts to cultural facts.

Indeed, there are neither child populations nor adult populations. Cultural or social Darwinism rests on a dangerous view of humankind and a mistaken concept of progress – seen as a linear sequence – whereas history shows that progress can be regressive and that bifurcations are many.

Marxism shares the same progress-oriented vision according to which cultures are but the expression of class struggle and history is moving towards ultimate progress.

Proponents of culturalism decline to set up a hierarchy of cultures in the perspective of permanent progress. They place cultures on the same level: each culture is a whole, which must be understood according to its own values and therefore from the inside. Comparing cultures is a meaningless exercise. Also, judging from the outside is dangerous since an observer is situated in his or her own culture and can never be completely objective. However, culturalism may lead to erroneous assumptions if it is seen as determinism, or if it leads one to think that cultures are bunker-like, unfathomable blocs among which communication and dialogue are truly impossible.

Therefore one should be aware of two pitfalls:
- One viewpoint denies differences for the benefit of a superior world civilization that would assert itself by levelling-off these differences. This is an abstract concept: 'a shallow formula' as per Lévi-Strauss, an impoverishment of humanity, a levelling down. Is this what lies in wait for us with standardized mass culture?
- The other viewpoint erects differences into impassable barriers. This viewpoint amounts to seeing humanity as a juxtaposition of different societies and cultures, without recourse to dialogue or mutual contributions. Each society or culture exists in isolation. This may be called the complex of the lighthouse keeper in unfriendly seas.

Human civilization is a rich concept, which the rainbow metaphor illustrates; *world civilization* is a shallow formula. Civilization implies dialogue between cultures, yet between cultures offering maximum diversity. The dialogue of cultures leads to mutual enrichment all the more as cultures are diversified. Cultural geography endeavours to understand such diversity by studying the distribution of cultures and cultural elements in time and space. This branch of human geography focuses on culture's role in major geographic issues.

5

Conclusion:
Is the territory (or place) a new paradigm
for human geography?[1]

Currently a debate about the territory is occurring in geography and also within the human sciences in general.[2] The concept is already enjoying a fair amount of success, as if geographers were going deeper – as if, digging under space, we had discovered the territory. Yet that discovery is somewhat disconcerting. After all, we may be giving too big a share to the irrational and still obscure foundations of humanity. Could the new paradigm be dangerous?

In this context, I wish to ask three questions:

- Does the discovery of territory herald the renewal of geographic thought? How does the territory-based approach differ from approaches based on spatial organization?
- Why the debate about territory? Why such concern? Some researchers want to do without it, but current events indicate that the territory is at the heart of all political stakes. Far from making it disappear, the world system is making the territory re-emerge in spite of itself, like a sort of spontaneous reaction or postmodern antidote.
- And, lastly, which kind of territory are we dealing with? Ethologists have their own definition ('the vital space, be it terrestrial, aquatic, or aerial, which an animal or group of animals defends as its exclusive possession'), lawyers have theirs, psychologists speak of it as the 'hidden dimension'. What do we

mean by territory in the human sciences, and human geography in particular? Are we always speaking of the same thing? The term must be defined: only then can we hope to enlighten a debate that has seemingly relied on fuzzy concepts and therefore paved the way for misunderstandings.

Misrepresenting the territory

There are two commensurate misrepresentations of the territory, not unlike the two sides of the same coin.

- Is there but one step from animal societies to human societies? Some authors have questioned the implicit *territorialism* of the notion of territory, equated with the terrorism of territory, itself associated with a limited vision of human nature; it leads directly to exacerbated nationalism, tribalism and ethnicism, with their de facto outcomes, including exclusion and 'purification'. In this case the territory is reduced to a 'frontier', to something that is used to generate warfare. The territory is seen as an imperative, a drive to conquer and defend one's domain.

- But to warn against this misrepresentation, or even to expose it, may lead to the inverse excess, which is to turn the territory into a *banal or lifeless concept*. The territory then appears as a 'minimalist' version, as if it had been cleaned off. It is now a *fragment of appropriated space*, a mesh of space which the community manages and organizes to ensure its reproduction and meet its vital needs. In this context one may speak of territorial planning. The territory becomes a technical concept that corresponds to a geographic function and is defined by the operational unity that the community assigns to it. Geographers speak of the '*production of a territory*'. In this case the territory is nothing but a prop – the projection in space of a social structure. The territory is seen as a district of the world system. Therefore it is no longer a frontier or an imperative – but by aiming to destroy its disquieting aspects, we may have changed its nature and made it so ordinary that it no longer means anything.

Space and territory

Does the territory stand against space? Geographers founded their discipline on the notion of region and the relation of human beings with the natural environment. In the 1960s they were won over by the concept of geographic space as an organized system whose determining factors were primarily economic.

Space is a physical reality, which buttresses relations of production. A geography of production structures ensues from it. Space produced by the world system or the world economy may be explained by the interplay of centres and peripheries; it is first and foremost a functional unit determined by economics. In the margins of the world system or, alternatively, 'underneath it', an anti-world[3] is revolving, a sort of world 'in reverse', which is defined and perceived in various ways.

This view perfects the very notion of spatial organization. Yet a number of researchers have been dissatisfied with it, in particular those who take an interest in the anti-world, the hidden and lesser-known spaces, the societies of the extreme periphery which do not abide by the world system's logic. These researchers have encountered other value systems. Working outside the space of the world system, they have unveiled its counterpart: the territory.

The territory may be defined as the reverse of space. It is based on an idea and often on an ideal, whereas space is material.[4] The territory is a worldview first and only secondly an organization. It refers more to representation than to functional purpose, but this does not mean that it is devoid of structures and substance. The territory has its own configurations, which vary according to societies and civilizations, and its substance is linked more to cultural, historical and political analysis than purely economic analysis. Not surprisingly, researchers started to investigate the territory to search for what space could not reveal. These pioneers looked at traditional societies where economic values are not primordial.

The territory is not necessarily the contrary of geographic space; it completes space. The territory is an *elsewhere* with two dimensions: a constituent element of a deeply rooted identity and, beyond it, a political stake.

Territory as identity

In its various spatial guises, the territory is inherent to all civilizations. The feeling of identification embodies itself in various places and geosymbols. Any given society has a territory: identity is linked to core places, which are also places of the heart. The feeling of identification is not one of simple and banal appropriation but an affective or even love-based relation. Places of identity often refer to the origins and are permeated by '*the undefinable grandeur of beginnings*', in Lévi-Strauss's words.

For Luc Bureau (1971), a geographer from Quebec, the territory is the *resonance between oneself and the world*.[5] And, I may add, it is the resonance of the earth within oneself. Thus the territory is something that is very sensual and primary but also very profound and magnificently elevated, '*opening the mind to the poetic, the sacred, and the infinite*', says Bureau. In this description we find the ambivalence of the territory, which is both land and poem.

The territory is first a space that allows for self-identification. It is based on a feeling and a vision. Its spatial form has little importance: it can vary to a great extent. The territory can even be imaginary or dreamed about, as is the case for diasporas. It can be a path, a constellation of places linked through walkabout trails as in the Aboriginal territories more sung than described by Bruce Chatwin,[6] a system of non-contiguous pasture land as among the Touareg, a road of canoes or a founding place as in Melanesia. The territory can be a heartland or a frontier or even a continual search for equilibrium between heartland and frontier. The territory is a fragment of space that gives roots to one's identity and unites those who share the same feeling.

In that sense, the territory is a linkage rather than a frontier.

Melanesians define themselves by identifying with networks of sacred places, and their actual frontiers are not lines but empty spaces without localities or inhabitants – that is, non-humanized spaces where the islanders never set foot. In that territorial system, the core counts more than the bounds. The territory is primarily a space of cultural identification or belonging; appropriation only comes later.

Territory as political stake

The territory as political space is quite different. Marked out by frontiers, which delineate a space of survival or power, this kind of territory is at the core of geopolitical challenges. There, space is defended, negotiated, coveted, lost, or else imagined. In it, nations play out their relations of domination. Nations fight for a territory, for a crest line such as the 'blue line of the Vosges',[7] or for the Falkland Islands,[8] even though they have no real economic stakes.

Compromises regarding goods, riches, or the space of production are always possible in case of conflict; but there can be no compromises as far as the territory is concerned. In that sense identity-related conflicts are tragic: the affective and symbolic force of territory is such that often no solution is available except for the 'might is right' option.

Geopolitical conflicts that result from the delineation of state frontiers are basically unresolved identity problems. Eventually they lead to wars all the more violent as identity-related issues have been denied, held in check and repressed for a long time. Recent warfare in the former Yugoslavia illustrates this process. The adversaries are fighting for territories buried for centuries in their memory and imagination, and it may not be so much their craving for space that motivates them as the assertion of their identity – wounded, long-muzzled and ailing. This is why adversaries in this conflict are so viscerally determined and why the search for a reasonable solution is so difficult.[9]

The territory is also the nexus of power; the master's eye is constantly present.[10] To carve and to control places within the territory is to dominate. Control of the land mediates the relations of authority between people and nation.

One may dislike or distrust the idea of territory because it upholds a notion of power or affirmation of identity that may be dangerous. Yet it is a tangible reality inscribed in space and time from which no one can free oneself. To deny the territory may bring about serious crises or excesses. The geographer Claude Raffestin wrote, perhaps on a day when he was pessimistic, '*space is the original prison; the territory is the prison that human beings give themselves*'. Is it a prison or a garden of happiness? The territory can probably be one and the other, and it does exist. One can find it.

The territory as place for ritual

I would like to complete this portrayal of territory on a more cultural note.

All told, what characterizes the territory is the presence of ritual. Traditional, modern, or postmodern humanity lives by means of rituals that reveal its hierarchies, express its values and buttress its beliefs, be they religious or not. A ritual calls for sacred places and, inversely, places call for rituals. The territory incorporates the various identity-related and political geosymbols that bind human communities and it does so through a network of high places. These high places are sanctuaries or the 'Holy of Holies'. They make the territory magical and as such are both dangerous and captivating, and also, in the final analysis, deeply human.

The territory begins with ritual. Indeed the territory is the most immediate of rituals. One feels it all the better when it is physical, for instance when one is walking – hence the significance of pilgrimages toward sanctuaries (secular or religious). Pilgrimages may be the first ritual practice ever invented by human beings or, to paraphrase Luc Bureau, their first resonance with the earth.

In short, the concept of territory bears on several research objectives. The territory is at the confluence of anthropology and geography. It serves as the foundation of historical, political and cultural geography. As a new paradigm, the territory fills a number of geographical, social and political functions but its reasons transcend these functions; they are in keeping with the universe of memory, representations and values.

Biography of Joël Bonnemaison

1940   2 August, born in Toulouse, France.

1951–59   High-school education in Paris.

1959–63   Attended University of Paris, majoring in Geography. Graduated with *licence* diploma. Editor of *Paraboles*, the periodical of Catholic students at the Sorbonne.

1963–64   Geography diploma with honours, University of Paris; thesis on country houses in Houdan, near Paris.

1965–66   Prepared doctoral thesis ('3rd cycle' thesis) in Madagascar; received ORSTOM research grant. Fulfilled national service obligations in Madagascar under ORSTOM authority.

1967   Recruited by ORSTOM (Scientific Research Institute for Development in Cooperation; now IRD, Research Institute for Development).

1968   Defended '3rd cycle' doctoral thesis on the Tsarahonenana *terroir* (Madagascar) at the University of Paris. Thesis accepted with honours.

1968–71   Posted at ORSTOM centre in Nouméa (New Caledonia). Did research on agrarian systems and social change in the New Hebrides archipelago; carried out comparative studies in the northern (Aoba, Maewo) and central (Tonga) islands.

1971–72   Posted at ORSTOM headquarters in Paris – scientific secretariat of the geography technical committee.

1972–75   Posted at ORSTOM centre in Nouméa. Did research on migration and urban growth in Vila and Luganville; and on land tenure and social transformation in Pentecost Island.

1976–81   Posted in Vila; created ORSTOM mission in the New Hebrides (now called Vanuatu). Did research on land tenure and socio-cultural change in the island of Tanna.

1981–85   Posted in France. Synthesized field research.

1985   Defended doctoral thesis (*doctorat d'Etat ès Lettres*), the highest-level degree within the French university system. Thesis accepted with honours by the University of Paris IV–Sorbonne. Thesis topic was 'The foundations of an identity: History, territory, and society in the Vanuatu archipelago'.

1985–87   Posted at Australian National University (ANU) as part of a research team working on development issues in the South Pacific. Carried out research missions in Fiji and Papua New Guinea.

1988–89   Posted at the ORSTOM Asia-Pacific headquarters in Nouméa.

1989–94   Posted at ORSTOM headquarters in Paris. Head of the SUD department (Society, Urbanization and Development).

1992   Part of the original group that launched the periodical *Géographie et cultures*, Paris

1994   Knight in the French National Order of Merit.

1994–97   Seconded by ORSTOM to University of Paris IV–Sorbonne as geography professor, cultural geography chair.

1996   Assistant director of the PRODIG research unit (Research Centre for the Management and Diffusion of Geographic Information), bringing together CNRS (National Centre for Scientific Research), the Universities of Paris I, Paris IV and Paris VII, and EPHE (École pratique des hautes études), an institute of higher education located in Paris.

1997   6 July, died in Nouméa. Bonnemaison was then a research director (highest level) at ORSTOM. He had requested a transfer to the University of Paris IV–Sorbonne as of 1 September 1997.

References

Agnew, J. A., 2002. *Place and Politics in Modern Italy*, Chicago, University of Chicago Press

Anderson, K., Domosh, M., Thrift, N., and Pile, S., (eds), 2003. *Handbook of Cultural Geography*, London, Sage Publications

'L'Approche culturelle', 1987. *L'Espace géographique*, special issue, 4

Baud, P., 1995. *Dictionnaire de la géographie*, Paris, Hatier

Béguin, F., 1995. *Le Paysage*, Paris, Flammarion

Bell, C., 1992. *Ritual Theory, Ritual Practice*, New York, Oxford University Press

Berdoulay, V., 1989. 'Place, Meaning, and Discourse in French-language Geography', in J. A. Agnew and J. S. Duncan (eds), *The Power of Place: Bringing Together Geographical and Sociological Imaginations*, London, Unwin Hyman

Berque, A., 1982. *Vivre l'espace au Japon*, Paris, PUF

Berque, A., 1984. 'Paysage-empreinte, paysage-matrice: éléments de problématique pour une géographie culturelle', *L'Espace géographique*, 19: 1, 33–4

Berque, A., 1986. *Le Sauvage et l'artifice. Les Japonais devant la nature*, Paris, Gallimard

Berque, A., 1990. *Médiance. De milieux en paysages*, Montpellier, Reclus

Berque, A., 1993. *Du geste à la cité. Formes urbaines et lien social au Japon*, Paris, Gallimard

Berque, A., 1994. *Cinq propositions pour une théorie du paysage*, Seyssel, Champ Vallon

Berque, A. 1995. *Les Raisons du paysage. De la Chine antique aux environnements de synthèse*, Paris, Hazan

Blanc-Pamard, C., 1995. 'Les lieux du corps. L'exemple des Hautes Terres centrales de Madagascar', in P. Claval and Singaravelou (eds), *Ethnogéographies*, Paris, L'Harmattan

Bloch, M., 1931. *Les Caractères originaux de l'histoire rurale française*, Oslo, Institut pour l'étude comparée des civilisations (new edition, Paris, A. Colin, 1988)

Blouet, B. W., (ed.), 1981. *The Origins of Academic Geography in the United States*, Hamden, Archon Books

Braudel, F., (ed.), 1985. *La Méditerranée. L'espace et l'histoire*, Paris, Flammarion (originally published 1977)

Braudel, F., 1993. *Grammaire des civilisations*, Paris, Flammarion (originally published 1963)

Breton, R., 1976. *Géographie des langues*, Paris, PUF

Breton, R., 1987. *Géographie des civilisations*, Paris, PUF

Brunhes, J., 1904. *L'Irrigation. Ses conditions géographiques, ses modes et son organisation*, Paris, Masson

Brunhes, J., 1920–26. *Géographie humaine de la France*, Paris, Plon, 2 vols

Brunhes, J., and Vallaux, C., 1921. *La Géographie de l'histoire. Géographie de la paix et de la guerre*, Paris, Alcan

Brunhes, J., 1947. *La Géographie humaine*, Paris, PUF (originally published 1910)

Bureau, L. 1971. *La Terre et moi*, Montreal, Boréal

Buttimer, A., 1983. *The Practice of Geography*, New York and London, Longman

Cambrézy, L., 1994. 'L'Interminable conquête, ou l'histoire d'un État propriétaire', *Géographie et cultures*, 10, 21–34

Chevalier, M., (ed.), 1989. *La Géographie de la créativité et de l'innovation*, Paris, Publications du département de géographie de l'université de Paris–Sorbonne

Clark, A., 1949. *The Invasion of New Zealand by People, Plants and Animals: The South Island*, New Brunswick, NJ, Rutgers University Press

Clastres, P., 1974. *La Société contre l'État*, Paris, Éditions de Minuit

Clastres, P., 1980. *Recherches d'anthropologie politique*, Paris, Le Seuil

Claval, P., 1973. *Principes de géographie sociale*, Paris, Genin

Claval, P., 1978. *Espace et pouvoir*, Paris, PUF

Claval, P., 1979. 'Régionalisme et consommation culturelle', *L'Espace géographique*, 4, 135–56

Claval, P., 1980. *Les Mythes fondateurs des sciences sociales*, Paris, PUF

Claval, P., 1984. *Géographie humaine et économique contemporaine*, Paris, PUF

Claval, P., 1990. *La Conquête de l'espace américain*, Paris, Flammarion

Claval, P., 1993. *La Géographie au temps de la chute des murs*, Paris, L'Harmattan

Claval, P., (ed.), 1993. *Autour de Vidal de la Blache. La formation de l'école française de géographie*, Paris, CNRS

Claval, P., 1994. *Géopolitique et géostratégie*, Paris, Nathan

Claval, P., 1995a. *Histoire de la géographie*, Paris, PUF

Claval, P., 1995b. *La Géographie culturelle*, Paris, Nathan

Claval, P., and Singaravelou, (eds), 1995. *Ethnogéographies*, Paris, L'Harmattan

Clayton, D., 2003. 'Critical Imperial and Colonial Geographies', in K. Anderson, M. Domosh, N. Thrift and S. Pile (eds), *Handbook of Cultural Geography*, London, Sage Publications, 354–68

Collignon, B., 1996. *Les Inuit. Ce qu'ils savent du territoire*, Paris, L'Harmattan

Condominas, G., 1980. *L'Espace social. À propos de l'Asie du Sud-Est*, Paris, Flammarion

Cosgrove, D., 1984. *Social Formation and Symbolic Landscape*, London, Croom Helm

Cosgrove, D., and Daniels, S., 1988. *The Iconography of Landscape*, Cambridge, Cambridge University Press

Cosgrove, D., and Jackson, P., 1989. 'New Directions in Cultural Geography', *Area*, 19, 95–101

Damasio, A., 2003. *Looking for Spinoza: Joy, Sorrow, and the Feeling Brain*, New York, Harcourt

Dardel, E., 1952. *L'Homme et la terre; nature de la réalité géographique*, Paris, PUF (new edition, Comité des travaux historiques et scientifiques, 1990)

Deffontaines, P., 1932, *L'Homme et la forêt*, Paris. Gallimard

Deffontaines, P., 1948. *Géographie et religions*, Paris, Gallimard

Deffontaines, P., 1972. *L'Homme et sa maison*, Paris, Gallimard

Delvert, J., 1961. *Le Paysan cambodgien*, Paris and The Hague, Mouton & Co. (new edition, L'Harmattan, 1994)

Demangeon, A., 1920a. 'L'Habitation rurale en France, Essai de classification des principaux types', *Annales de géographie*, 29, 352–75

Demangeon, A., 1920b. *Le Déclin de l'Europe*, Paris, A. Colin

Demangeon, A., 1922. *L'Empire britannique*, Paris, A. Colin

Demangeon, A., 1927a. *Belgique, Pays-Bas, Luxembourg*, Paris, A. Colin

Demangeon, A., 1927b. *Les Îles britanniques*, Paris, A. Colin

Descola, P., 1993. *Les Lances du crépuscule: relations Jivaros. Haute Amazonie*, Paris, Plon

Dion, R., 1934. *Essai sur la formation du paysage rural français*, Tours, Arrault

Dion, R., 1990. *Le Paysage et la vigne. Essai de géographie historique*, Paris, Payot

Dumézil, G., 1977. *Mythe et épopée*, Paris, Gallimard

Duncan, J. S., and Ley, D., 1993. 'Introduction', in J. S. Duncan and D. Ley (eds), *Place/Culture/Representation*, London, Routledge

Dupont, L., 1998. 'L'Effet Bonnemaison', in D. Guillaud, M. Seysset and A. Walter (eds), *Le Voyage inachevé ... à Joël Bonnemaison*, Paris, Éditions de l'ORSTOM-PRODIG, 105–7

Durand, M.-F., Lévy, J., and Retaillé, D., 1992. *Le Monde. Espaces et systèmes*, Paris, Presses de la Fondation nationale des sciences politiques and Dalloz

Eliade, M., 1963. *Aspects du mythe*, Paris, Gallimard

Eliade, M., 1965. *Le Sacré et le profane*, Paris, Gallimard (originally published 1957)

Eliade, M., 1972. *Religions australiennes*, Paris, Payot

Elkin, A. P., 1967. *Les Aborigènes australiens*, Paris, Gallimard (originally published 1938)

Entrikin, J. N., 1991. *The Betweenness of Place: Towards a Geography of Modernity*, Baltimore, Johns Hopkins University Press

Flatrès, P., 1986. *La Bretagne*, Paris, PUF

Foucher, M., (ed.), 1993. *Fragments d'Europe*, Paris, Fayard

Frémont, A., 1976. *La Région, espace vécu*, Paris, PUF

Frémont, A., 1981. *Paysans de Normandie*, Paris, Flammarion

Frobenius, L., 1952. *Histoire de la civilisation africaine*, Paris, NRF, Gallimard

Gade, D. W., 1976. 'L'Optique culturelle dans la géographie américaine', *Annales de géographie*, 85: 472, 672–93

Gallais, J., 1967. *Le Delta intérieur du Niger, Étude de géographie régionale*, Dakar, IFAN, 2 vols

Gallais, J., 1984. *Hommes du Sahel. Espaces-temps et pouvoirs. Delta intérieur du Niger 1960–1980*, Paris, Flammarion

Gallais, J., 1989. *Une géographie politique de l'Ethiopie. Le poids de l'État*, Paris, Economica

Gallais, J., 1994. *Les Tropiques. Terres de risques et de violences*, Paris, Armand Colin

'Géographie historique', 1994. *Hérodote*, special issue, 74–5

Gottmann, J., 1947. *La Politique des États et leur géographie*, Paris, Armand Colin

Gourou, P. 1936. *Les Paysans du delta tonkinois. Étude de géographie humaine*, Paris, Éditions d'Art et d'Histoire

Gourou, P., 1966. *Les Pays tropicaux*, Paris, PUF (originally published 1947)

Gourou, P., 1970. *L'Afrique*, Paris, Hachette

Gourou, P., 1971. *L'Asie*, Paris, Hachette

Gourou, P., 1972. *La Terre et l'homme en Extrême-Orient*, Paris, Flammarion

Gourou, P., 1973. *Pour une géographie humaine*, Paris, Flammarion

Gourou, P., 1982. *Terres de bonne espérance: le monde tropical*, Paris, Plon

Gourou, P., 1986. *Riz et civilisation*, Paris, Fayard

Gramsci, A., 1974–83. *Écrits politiques*, Paris, Gallimard, 3 vols

Grousset, R., 1990. *Bilan de l'histoire*, Paris, Desclée de Brouwer

Guest, H., 2002. 'Mapping Differences: Representations of Pacific Islands in Cook's Second Voyage', paper presented at the Conference on Tropical Views and Exchanges: Images of the Tropical World. National Maritime Museum, London, 12–13 July. The author is at the Department of English, University of York, England

Guiart, J., 1996. 'Land Tenure and Hierarchies in Eastern Melanesia', *Pacific Studies*, 19: 1, 21–9.

Guillaud, D., Seysset, M., and Walter, A., (eds), 1998. *Le Voyage inachevé ... à Joël Bonnemaison*, Paris, Éditions de l'ORSTOM-PRODIG

Gupta, A., and Ferguson, J., (eds), 1997. *Culture, Power, Place: Explorations in Critical Anthropology*, Durham, NC, Duke University Press

Harvey, D., 1989. *The Condition of Postmodernity. An Enquiry into the Origins of Cultural Change*, Cambridge, B. Blackwell

Haudricourt, A. G., and Hédin, L., 1943. *L'Homme et les plantes cultivées*, Paris, Gallimard

Haudricourt, A. G., 1987. *La Technologie, science humaine*, Paris, Maison des sciences de l'homme

Haudry, J., 1981. *Les Indo-Européens*, Paris, PUF

Hudson, J. C., 1972. *Geographical Diffusion Theory*, Evanston, Northwestern University, Department of Geography

Laponce, J., 1984. *Langue et territoire*, Quebec, Presses de l'université Laval

Latouche, S., 1991. *La Planète des naufragés. Essai sur l'après-développement*, Paris, La Découverte

Leenhardt, M., 1937. *Gens de la Grande Terre*, Paris, Gallimard

Leenhardt, M., 1947. *Do Kamo: la personne et le mythe dans le monde mélanésien*, Paris, Gallimard

Leroi-Gourhan, A., 1948–50. *Évolution et techniques*, Paris, Albin Michel, 2 vols

Lévi-Strauss, C., 1949. *Les Structures élémentaires de la parenté*, Paris, PUF

Lévi-Strauss, C., 1952. *Race et histoire*, Paris, UNESCO (new edition, Gallimard, 1987)

Lévi-Strauss, C., 1955. *Tristes Tropiques*, Paris, Plon

Lévi-Strauss, C., 1962. *La Pensée sauvage*, Paris, Plon

Lévi-Strauss, C., (ed.), 1977. *L'Identité*, Paris, Grasset and Fasquelle

Ley, D., (ed.), 1983. *Humanistic Geography: Problems and Prospects. Place, Culture, Representation*, Chicago, Routledge

Lindstrom, L., 1993. *Cargo Cult: Strange Stories of Desire from Melanesia and Beyond*, Honolulu, University of Hawaii Press

Lowenthal, D., 1976. *Geographies of the Mind: Essays in Historical Geosophy in Honor of John Kirkland Wright*, New York, Oxford University Press

MacColla, F., 1945. *And the Cock Crew*, Glasgow, William McClellan (reissued Edinburgh, Canongate, 1995)

Malinowski, B., 1963. *Les Argonautes du Pacifique occidental*, Paris, Gallimard (originally published 1922)

Malinowski, B., 1974. *Les Jardins de corail*, Paris, Maspero (originally published 1935)

Massey, D., 1999. 'Spaces of Politics', in D. Massey, J. Allen and P. Sarre (eds), *Human Geography Today*, Cambridge, Polity Press

Mitchell, D., 1995. 'There's No Such Thing as Culture: Towards a Reconceptualization of the Idea of Culture in Geography', *Transactions of the Institute of British Geographers*, 20, 102–16

Mondada, L, and Söderström, O., 1993. 'Parcours à travers la géographie culturelle contemporaine', *Géographie et cultures*, 8, 71–82

Olsson, G., 1979. *Philosophy of Geography*, Dordrecht, D. Reidel

'Paysage et cultures', 1977. *Cahiers de géographie du Québec*, special issue, 21: 53–4

Pélissier, P., 1966. *Les Paysans du Sénégal. Les civilisations agraires du Cayor à la Casamance*, Saint-Yrieix, Fabrègue

Pélissier, P., 1995. *Campagnes africaines en devenir*, Paris, Arguments

Philibert, J.-M., and Rodman, M., 1998. 'Joël Bonnemaison, profession: ethnographe', in D. Guillaud, M. Seysset and A. Walter (eds), *Le voyage inachevé ... à Joël Bonnemaison*, Paris, Éditions de l'ORSTOM-PRODIG, 97–101

Pinchemel, P. and G., 1988. *La Face de la terre*, Paris, Armand Colin

Pitte, J.-R., 1983. *Histoire du paysage français*, Paris, Tallandier, 2 vols

Pitte, J.-R., 1986. *Terres de Castanide. Hommes et paysages du châtaignier de l'Antiquité à nos jours*, Paris, Fayard

Pitte, J.-R., (ed.), 1995. *Géographie historique et culturelle de l'Europe. Hommage au Professeur Xavier de Planhol*, Presses de l'université de Paris–Sorbonne

Planhol, X. de, 1957. *Le Monde islamique. Essai de géographie religieuse*, Paris, PUF

Planhol, X. de, 1968. *Les Fondements géographiques de l'histoire de l'Islam*, Paris, Flammarion

Planhol, X. de, 1988. *Géographie historique de la France*, Paris, Fayard

Planhol, X. de, 1993. *Les Nations du Prophète. Manuel de géographie politique musulmane*, Paris, Fayard

Planhol, X. de, 1995. *L'Eau de neige, le tiède et le frais. Histoire et géographie des boissons fraîches*, Paris, Fayard

Poirier, S., 1996. *Les Jardins du nomade. Cosmologie, territoire et personne dans le désert occidental australien*, Münster, LIT Verlag

Raffestin, C., 1977. 'Paysage et territorialité', *Cahiers de géographie de Québec*, 53–4, 123–34

Raffestin, C., 1980. *Pour une géographie du pouvoir*, Paris, Litec

Ratzel, F., 1880. *Kulturgeographie der Vereinigten Staaten von Nord-Amerika unter besonderer Berücksichtigung der wirtschaftlischen Verhältnisse*, Munich, Oldenburg

Ratzel, F., 1881–91. *Anthropogeographie, oder Grundzüge der Anwendung der Erdkunde auf die Geschichte*, Stuttgart, Englehorn, 2 vols

Ratzel, F., 1885–88. *Völkerkunde*, Leipzig, Bibliographisches Institut, 3 vols

Ratzel, F., 1897. *Politische Geographie*, Munich and Leipzig, Oldenburg (2nd edition, Eugen Oberhummer, 1923), translated 1988, Éditions régionales européennes

Reclus, E., 1982. *L'Homme et la terre*, Paris, La Découverte, 2 vols (new edition)

Rostlund, E., 1955. *Outline of Cultural Geography*, Berkeley, University of California Press

Rostow, W. W., 1962. *Les Étapes de la croissance économique*, Paris, Seuil

Sack, R. D., 1997. *Homo Geographicus: A Framework for Action, Awareness, and Moral Concern*, Baltimore, Johns Hopkins University Press

Sack, R. D., 2003. *A Geographical Guide to the Real and the Good*, New York, Routledge

Sanguin, A.-L., 1993. *Vidal de la Blache. Un génie de la géographie*, Paris, Belin

Sauer, C. O., 1925. 'The Morphology of Landscape', *University of California, Publications in Geography*, 2: 2, 19–54

Sauer, C. O., 1927. 'Recent Developments in Cultural Geography', in E. C. Hayes, *Recent Developments in the Social Sciences*, Philadelphia, Lippincott, 154–212

Sauer, C. O., 1947. 'Early Relations of Man to Plants', *Geographical Review*, 37: 1, 1–25

Sauer, C. O., 1963. *Land and Life. A Selection from the Writings of Carl Ortwin Sauer*, Berkeley, University of California Press

Sautter, G., 1966. *De l'Atlantique au fleuve Congo, une géographie du souspeuplement. République du Congo, République Gabonaise*, Paris and The Hague, Mouton, 2 vols

Sautter, G., 1968. *Les Structures agraires en Afrique tropicale*, Paris, C.D.U.

Sautter, G., 1979. 'Le Paysage comme connivence', *Hérodote*, 16, 40–67

Sautter, G., 1993. *Parcours d'un géographe. Des paysages aux ethnies, de la brousse à la ville, de l'Afrique au monde*, Paris, Arguments, 2 vols

Scheibling, J., 1994. *Qu'est-ce que la géographie?*, Paris, Hachette

Schumpeter, J., 1935. *Théorie de l'évolution économique*, Paris, Dalloz (originally published 1911)

Sevin, O., 1992. 'Java entre hindouisme et islam', *Géographie et cultures*, 3, 89–103

Sevin, O., 1993. *L'Indonésie*, Paris, PUF

Siegfried, A., 1913. *Tableau politique de la France de l'Ouest sous la Troisième République*, Paris, Armand Colin

Siegfried, A., 1952. *Géographie politique des cinq continents*, Paris, La Passerelle

Sorre, M., 1943. *Les Fondements biologiques de la géographie humaine. Essai d'une écologie de l'homme*, Paris, Armand Colin

Sorre, M., 1948. 'La Notion de genre de vie et sa valeur actuelle', *Annales de géographie*, 57, 97–108 and 193–204

Sorre, M., 1957. *Rencontres entre la sociologie et la géographie*, Paris, Rivière

Spencer, J., 1978. 'The Growth of Cultural Geography', *American Behavioral Scientist*, 22, 79–92

Spencer, J. E., and Thomas, W. L., 1969. *Cultural Geography. An Evolutionary Introduction to our Humanized Earth*, New York, John Wiley

Spengler, O., 1931–33. *Le Déclin de l'Occident*, Paris, Gallimard (new edition 1993, 2 vols)

Taillard, C., 1981. 'Diversité des définitions et différenciation des pratiques géographiques: contribution au débat sur la culture', *L'Espace géographique*, 4, 263–9

Thomas, N., 1996. '"On the Varieties of the Human Species": Forster's Comparative Ethnology', in N. Thomas, H. Guest and M. Dettelbach (eds), *Johann Reinhold Forster, 'Observations Made During a Voyage Round the World'*, Honolulu, University of Hawaii Press

Trochet, J.-R., 1993. *Aux origines de la France rurale. Outils, pays et paysages*, Paris, CNRS

Tuan, Y.-F., 1977. *Space and Place: The Perspective of Experience*, London, Methuen

Tuan, Y.-F., 1982. *Segmented Worlds and Self: Group Life and Individual Consciousness*, Minneapolis, University of Minnesota Press

Vidal de la Blache, P., 1889. *États et nations de l'Europe. Autour de la France*, Paris, Delagrave

Vidal de la Blache, P., 1903. *Tableau de la géographie de la France*, Paris, Hachette

Vidal de la Blache, P., 1913. 'Des caractères distinctifs de la géographie', *Annales de géographie*, 22, 289–99

Vidal de la Blache, P., 1922. *Principes de géographie humaine*, Paris, Armand Colin (new edition, Paris, Utz, 1995)

Waddell, E., 1976. 'Valeurs religieuses et rapports homme-milieu. Perspectives de l'écologie culturelle anglo-américaine', *Protée*, 11–17

Waddell, E., 1996. 'Du sang dans le Tanoa ... ou l'appel du Grand Océan', *Cahiers de géopoétique*, 5, 61–84

Waddell, Eric, 1999. 'Rootedness and Travels: The Intellectual Journey of Joël Bonnemaison', *Contemporary Pacific*, 11: 1, 176–85

Wagner, P. L., and Mikesell, M. W. (eds), 1962. *Readings in Cultural Geography*, Chicago, University of Chicago Press

See also the journal *Géographie et cultures* (1992–present).

Works by Joël Bonnemaison

Books

1975: *Nouvelles-Hébrides* (photos: B. Hermann), Papeete, Éditions du Pacifique, 128 pp. (English version published as *The New Hebrides*, 1975, 2nd edition published as *Vanuatu*, 1980)

1976: *Tsarahonenana: des riziculteurs de montagne dans l'Ankaratra (Madagascar)*, Atlas des structures agraires à Madagascar, no. 3, Paris, ORSTOM, 97 pp.

1977: *Système de migration et croissance urbaine à Port-Vila et Luganville (Nouvelles-Hébrides)*, Travaux et documents de l'ORSTOM, no. 60, Paris, ORSTOM, 97 pp.

1986a: *La Dernière île*, Paris, Arléa, ORSTOM, 421 pp.

1986b: *Les Fondements d'une identité: territoire, histoire et société dans l'archipel de Vanuatu (Mélanésie)*, Travaux et documents de l'ORSTOM, no. 201, Paris, ORSTOM, 2 vols (vol. 1: *L'Arbre et la pirogue*, 540 pp.; vol. 2: *Les Hommes-lieux et les hommes-flottants*, 618 pp.)

1988: *Atlas des îles et États du Pacifique sud* (with B. Antheaume), Montpellier, GIP Reclus and Paris, Publisud, 126 pp.

1994: *The Tree and the Canoe: History and Ethnogeography of Tanna* (translated and adapted by Josée Pénot-Demetry), Honolulu, University of Hawaii Press, 368 pp.

1995: *Asie du Sud-Est, Océanie* (with B. Antheaume, M. Bruneau and C. Taillard), *Géographie universelle*, vol. 7, Paris, Belin Reclus, 480 pp.

1996a: *Gens de pirogue et gens de la terre. Les fondements géographiques d'une identité: l'archipel du Vanuatu*, Paris, ORSTOM (revised edition of *L'Arbre et la pirogue*)

1996b: *Une aire pacifique?* (with B. Antheaume), Documentation photographique, Paris, La Documentation française, 44 pp., including 15 slides with comments

1996c: *Vanuatu Océanie. Arts des îles de cendre et de corail* (with K. Huffman, C. Kaufmann and D. Tryon), Paris, ORSTOM, RMN, 384 pp.

1997a: *Arts of Vanuatu* (with K. Huffman, C. Kaufmann and D. Tryon), Honolulu, University of Hawaii Press, 320 pp.

1997b: *Les Gens des lieux. Histoire et géosymboles d'une société enracinée: Tanna. Les fondements géographiques d'une identité: l'archipel du Vanuatu*, Paris, ORSTOM, 562 pp. (revised edition of *Tanna: les hommes-lieux*)

1999: *Le Territoire, lien ou frontière?*, 1995 colloquium report (with L. Cambrézy and L. Quinty-Bourgeois), Paris, L'Harmattan, 2 vols (vol. 1: *Les Territoires de l'identité*; vol. 2, *La Nation et le territoire*)

Book chapters

1972: 'New Hebrides, Map of Land Use with Summary', in *World Atlas of Agriculture*, Milan, 629–31

1978a: 'Custom and Money: Integration or Breakdown in Melanesian Systems of Production', in E. K. Fisk (ed.), *The Adaptation of Traditional Agriculture: Socio-Economic Problems of Urbanization*, Canberra, Development Studies Centre, 25–45

1978b: 'Man mo garen long Niu-Hebridis: olgeta rod blong prisen long fasin long Kastom', in R. Brunton, J. Lynch and D. Tryon (eds), *Man, languis mo Kastom long Niu-Hebridis*, Canberra, Development Studies Centre, 31–40 (work in Melanesian pidgin)

1980: 'Moving Food in Rural Areas: the Case Study of Central Pentecost', in G. Ward, T. Mac Gee and D. Drakakis-Smith (eds), *New Hebridean Systems of Food Distribution*, Canberra, Development Studies Centre, 150–78

1981a: 'La Terre au Vanuatu: aspects sociaux et culturels', in P. Larmour (ed.), *Systèmes fonciers au Vanuatu*, Suva, Fiji, University of the South Pacific, 19–26

1981b: 'Les Migrations en Nouvelle-Calédonie' (with J. Fages and J.-C. Roux), in *Atlas de la Nouvelle-Calédonie et dépendances*, Paris, ORSTOM, plate 39

1983: 'Du terroir au territoire: des problèmes de développement à une géographie culturelle', in *Profession géographe, pratique de la recherche tropicale*, Paris, ORSTOM, 99–106

1984a: 'Les Jardins magiques. Le géosystème de l'horticulture vivrière dans une île mélanésienne du Pacifique Sud', in *Le Développement rural en question*, Paris, ORSTOM, 461–82

1984b: 'Social and Cultural Aspects of Land Tenure', in P. Larmour (ed.), *Land Tenure in Vanuatu*, Suva, Fiji, University of the South Pacific, 1–5

1985: 'Territorial Control and Mobility within Vanuatu Societies', in K. M. Prothero and M. Chapman (eds), *Circulation and Population Movement: Substance and Concepts from the Melanesian Case*, London, Routledge & Kegan Paul, 57–79

1988a: 'L'Expérience de la frontière: la nature et la société en Australie', in G. Ordonnaud and A. Sérieyx (eds), *L'Australie 88: bicentenaire ou naissance*, Paris, France-Empire, 25–51

1988b: 'Le Nord ou la frontière dangereuse', in G. Ordonnaud and A. Sérieyx (eds), *L'Australie 88: bi-centenaire ou naissance*, Paris, France-Empire, 353–61

1989a: 'L'Espace réticulé: commentaires sur l'idéologie géographique', in B. Antheaume, C. Blanc-Pamard, J.-L. Chaleard, et al (eds), *Tropiques, lieux et liens*, Paris, ORSTOM, 500–10

1989b: 'Le Sens de la route: valeurs de l'enracinement et du voyage en Mélanésie', in *Migrations et identité*, Nouméa, CORAIL, vol. 1, 113–16

1989c: 'Papouasie-Nouvelle-Guinée', in *Encyclopædia Universalis*, Paris, 458–62

1990: 'Fiji' and 'Vanuatu', in *Encyclopædia Universalis, thesaurus*, Paris

1991a: 'Le Taro-roi: une horticulture d'abondance dans l'archipel du Vanuatu (Mélanésie)', in *Aspects du monde tropical et asiatique, hommage à Jean Delvert*, Paris, Presses de l'université de France, 518–23

1991b: 'Océanie', in M. Izard and P. Bonte (eds), *Dictionnaire de l'ethnologie et de l'anthropologie*, Paris, Presses universitaires Paris–Sorbonne, 305–15

1993: 'Australie', in *Encyclopédie Axis*, Paris, Hachette

1996a: 'Gens de l'igname et gens du taro', in *Mémoire de pierre, mémoire d'homme, hommage à José Garanger*, Paris, Publications de la Sorbonne, 389–404

1996b: 'L'Océanie', in Thierry Paquot (ed.), *Le Monde des villes, panorama urbain de la planète*, Paris, Éditions Complexe, 339–44

1996c: 'Les Mots de la terre sacrée', in J.-F. Vincent, D. Dory and R. Verdier (eds), *La Construction religieuse du territoire*, Paris, L'Harmattan, 66–73

1996d: 'La Métaphore de l'arbre et de la pirogue', in *Vanuatu Océanie. Arts des îles de cendre et de corail*, Paris, ORSTOM, RMN, 34–8

1996e: 'Le Tissu de nexus', in *Vanuatu Océanie. Arts des îles de cendre et de corail*, Paris, ORSTOM, RMN, 176–7

1996f: 'La Coutume ou les formes du pouvoir politique traditionnel au Vanuatu', in *Vanuatu Océanie. Arts des îles de cendre et de corail*, Paris, ORSTOM, RMN, 212–29

1997: 'L'Extrême-Occident dans l'oeil du cyclone' (with Eric Waddell), in Joël Bonnemaison and Jean Freyss (eds), *Le Tiers-monde insulaire, nations, aides, espaces*, Paris, Institut d'études du développement économique et social, 13–34

2000: 'Tsarahonenana ou la route circulaire. Postface', in C. Blanc-Pamard and H. Rakoto Ramiarantsoa (eds), *Le Terroir et son double. Tsarahonenana (1966–1992) Madagascar*, Paris, IRD, 'À travers champs' collection, 194–207

Articles

1971a: 'Des riziculteurs d'altitude: Tsarahonenana', *Études rurales*, special issue, 37–9, 326–44

1971b: 'Le Peuplement des hauts de l'Ankaratra', *Revue de géographie de Madagascar*, 14, 33–69

1972a: 'Système de grades et différences régionales en Aoba', *Cahiers ORSTOM, série sciences humaines*, special issue on Oceania in transition, IX: 1, 87–108

1972b: 'Description et classification des biens traditionnels dans la région Nord-Est d'Aoba', *Cahiers ORSTOM, série sciences humaines*, special issue on Oceania in transition, IX: 1, 121–4

1972c: 'Prise de grades en Aoba', *Cahiers ORSTOM, série sciences humaines*, special issue on Oceania in transition, IX: 1, 109–20

1974a: 'Changements dans la vie rurale et mutations migratoires aux Nouvelles-Hébrides', *Cahiers ORSTOM, série sciences humaines*, IX: 3–4, 259–86

1974b: 'Espaces et paysages agraires dans le nord des Nouvelles-Hébrides: l'exemple des îles d'Aoba et de Maewo', *Journal de la société des océanistes*, 44, 163–232 and 45, 259–81

1975: 'L'Expérience de l'office du logement à Port-Moresby, Papouasie-Nouvelle-Guinée', *Journal de la société des océanistes*, 48, 361–4

1976: 'Circular Migration and Wild Migration in the New Hebrides', *South Pacific Bulletin*, 26: 4, 7–13

1977: 'The Impact of Population Patterns and Cash Cropping in Urban Migrations in New Hebrides', *Pacific Viewpoint*, 18: 2, 119–32

1979a: 'Le Volcan, les cocotiers, le bocage: la région du volcan Yasür à Tanna', *Revue de photo-interprétation*, special issue on rural landscapes, 3, 35–42

1979b: 'Les Voyages et l'enracinement: formes de fixation et de mobilité dans la société traditionnelle des Nouvelles-Hébrides', *L'Espace géographique*, 8: 4, 303–18

1980: 'Espace géographique et identité culturelle en Vanuatu', *Journal de la société des océanistes*, 36: 68, 181–8

1981: 'Voyage autour du territoire', *L'Espace géographique*, special issue on cultural geography, 10: 4, 249–62

1984: 'Recherches géographiques dans le Tiers-monde: libres réflexions sur une pratique de la géographie à l'ORSTOM' (with B. Antheaume, A. Lericollais and J.-Y. Marchal), *L'Espace géographique*, 13: 4, 353–60

1985a: 'De la nature de l'espace à l'espace de la culture: images sociales et culturelles d'un espace insulaire', *L'Espace géographique*, 14: 1, 33

1985b: 'Les Lieux de l'identité: vision du passé et identité culturelle dans les îles du centre et du sud de Vanuatu', *Cahiers ORSTOM, série sciences humaines*, special issue on anthropology and history, 21: 1, 151–70

1985c: 'The Tree and the Canoe: Roots and Mobility in Vanuatu Societies', *Pacific Viewpoint*, 25: 2, 117–51 (reprinted in *Pacific*

Viewpoint, special issue: Mobility and Identity in the Island Pacific, 26: 1 (1986), 30–62)

1985d: 'Un certain refus de l'État: autopsie d'une tentative de sécession en Mélanésie', *International Political Science Review*, 6: 2, 230–47

1985e: 'Vanuatu: la coutume et l'indépendance', *Hérodote*, special issue on French-speaking islands, 37–8, 145–61

1986a: 'À propos de l'affaire Greenpeace ... Là-bas à l'ouest de l'Occident: l'Australie et la Nouvelle-Zélande ...', *Hérodote*, 40, 126–39

1986b: 'Passions et misères d'une société coloniale: les plantations au Vanuatu entre 1920 et 1980', *Journal de la société des océanistes*, special issue on plantations in the Pacific, 82–3, 65–84

1987: 'Le Roc des Aborigènes', *L'Espace géographique*, field notes, 16: 3, 216

1990a: 'L'ORSTOM: géographes sans frontières', *Intergéo bulletin*, 99, 20–3

1990b: 'Les Hommes à perruque, balade à Huli en Papouasie-Nouvelle-Guinée', *L'Espace géographique*, 19: 3, 222–3

1990c: 'Political Review Polynesia: Wallis and Futuna', *The Contemporary Pacific*, 2: 1, 176–8

1990d: 'Political Review Melanesia: Vanuatu' (with E. Huffer), *The Contemporary Pacific*, 2: 1, 373, 375, 377

1991a: 'Le Développement est un exotisme', *Ethnies*, 13, La fiction et la feinte, développement et peuples autochtones, 12–17

1991b: 'Magic Gardens in Tanna', *Pacific Studies*, 14: 4, 71–89

1991c: 'Vivre dans l'île: une approche de l'îléité océanienne', *L'Espace géographique*, 2, 119–25

1992: 'Le Territoire enchanté. Croyances et territorialité en Mélanésie', *Géographie et cultures*, 3, 71–88

1993a: 'Preface', in E. Huffer, *Grands hommes et petites îles: la politique extérieure de Fidji, Tonga et Vanuatu*, Paris, ORSTOM

1993b: 'Around Territories: Two Decades of Espace géographique: An Anthology', *L'Espace géographique*, 22: 5, Espaces – modes d'emploi, 205–20

1993c: 'Porter sur la nature un regard amical', in 'Savoirs, Une terre en renaissance: les semences du développement durable', ORSTOM, *Le Monde diplomatique*, 2, 55–6

1993d: 'Sociocultural Development Issues: State Needs and Stateless Societies in the Pacific Islands' (with Paul de Deckker), in *Development and Planning in Small Island Nations of the Pacific*, selected papers from the International Conference on Multilevel Development and Planning in Pacific Island Countries, Nuku'alofa, Tonga, 10–13 January 1990, Nagoya, United Nations Centre for Regional Development, 19–26

1997a: 'L'Arbre est la métaphore de l'homme', in *Littératures francophones d'Asie et du Pacifique (anthologie)*, Paris, Nathan, 136–9

1997b: 'La Sagesse des îles', in A. L. Sanguin (ed.), *Vivre dans une île: une géopolitique des insularités*, Paris, L'Harmattan, pp. 121–9

1997c: 'Le Lien territorial, entre frontières et identités' (with L. Cambrézy), *Géographie et cultures*, 20, 7–18

1997d: 'Les Aspects théoriques de la question du territoire' (with L. Cambrézy), foreword to *Géographie et cultures*, special issue on territory, 20, 3–5

1997e: 'Les Lieux de l'identité: vision du passé et identité culturelle dans les îles du sud et du centre de Vanuatu (Mélanésie)', reprint of 1985b

1997f: 'Tsarahonenana 25 ans après: un terroir "où il fait toujours bon vivre". Les ressorts d'un système agraire, Vakinankaratra (Madagascar)' (with C. Blanc-Pamard and H. Rakoto Ramiarantsoa), in C. Blanc-Pamard and J. Boutrais (eds), *Thème et variations. Nouvelles recherches rurales au Sud*, Paris, ORSTOM, 25–61

Tributes to Joël Bonnemaison published after his death

1998: D. Guillaud, M. Seysset and A. Walter (eds), *Le Voyage inachevé ... à Joël Bonnemaison*, Paris, ORSTOM, PRODIG, 776 pp.

1998: *B. Comme Big Man. Hommage à Joël Bonnemaison*, Paris, Grafigéo 4, PRODIG, 130 pp.

Notes

1 Introduction

1 This chapter reproduces an ORSTOM research report by J. Bonne-maison. – Trans.
2 *Un 'lieu préalable'*.
3 *Études de terroir*. *Terroir* means (1) any small rural area that has an influ-ence on its inhabitants; (2) the specific area within a given region that supplies a characteristic food or wine. An example of recent *terroir*-related research is Emmanuelle Vaudour, 'The Quality of Grapes and Wine in Relation to Geography: Notions of *Terroir* at Various Scales', *Journal of Wine Research*, 13: 2 (2002), 117–41. – Trans.
4 ORSTOM (Scientific Research Institute for Development in Coopera-tion) became IRD (Research Institute for Development) in 1999.
5 The word in the French text is 'men'. Throughout I have translated 'men' as 'human beings' unless otherwise noted. – Trans.
6 Paris, ORSTOM, 1986b
7 In French the term means both the bastion-like core of a territory and a battlefield. One of Bonnemaison's favourite expressions. – Trans.
8 Paris, Arléa, ORSTOM, 1986a.
9 Honolulu, University of Hawaii Press, 1994.
10 The sentence in the original text is in English. – Trans.
11 B. Antheaume and J. Bonnemaison (eds), *Atlas des îles et États du Paci-fique sud*, Montpellier, GIP Reclus and Paris, Publisud, 1988. The atlas, the first of its kind, included contributions by anglophone and franco-phone geographers. – Trans.
12 Paris, Belin, Reclus, 1995a.

2 The revival of the cultural approach

1 A writer who was part of the Resistance movement during Word War II and became minister of cultural affairs under Charles de Gaulle. – Trans.
2 This sentence summarizes two key points. Gramsci (1891–1937), a founder of the Italian Communist Party, attacked existing cultural forms and the society that created them but also asserted that a workers' civilization would create new cultural forms, thereby upholding the sub-versive power of culture. – Trans.
3 An allusion to Bonnemaison's field studies in Madagascar and the New Hebrides from the 1960s to the 1980s. – Trans.

4 And a landscape with which they are in communion (*en connivence*). Cf. Gilles Sautter's article in *Hérodote* (1979).

5 'Milieu represents a combination of places and areas both natural and culture-bound, collective and individual, subjective and objective, physical and phenomenological, material and ideological. *Médiance* is that which gives meaning to milieu in a descriptive and prescriptive sense' (Berque 1986, 162). Source: Bonnemaison, *The Tree and the Canoe*, 345. – Trans.

6 Bonnemaison uses the term *genius*. – Trans.

7 The original meaning of *Landschaft* is 'region'. Therefore *Landschaft* is not an exact synonym of 'landscape', and *Landschaftskunde* falls midway between 'landscape science' and 'regional geography'.

8 Karl Ernst Haushofer (1869–1946), German army officer, political geographer and leading proponent of geopolitics in his journal *Zeitschrift für Geopolitik*, in which he gave a geopolitical rationale to the international claims of Germany. The Nazis adopted his theories for their own purposes. – Trans.

9 The most prestigious training school for teachers in France. – Trans.

10 'A form of livelihood functionally characteristic of a human group', as defined in R. J. Johnston et al. (eds), *The Dictionary of Human Geography*, 3rd edition, Cambridge, MA, and Oxford, Blackwell Publishers, 1994. – Trans.

11 Paris, Gallimard, 1932, 1972.

12 With characteristic enthusiasm, Bonnemaison strings several metaphors about the emergence of cultural geography: flowering, starting the race, California as cradle, and so on. – Trans.

13 *Kava*: a traditional beverage in Melanesia, extracted from the plant *Piper methysticum*. – Trans.

14 Brittany and Gascony, in the southwest, were Bonnemaison's favourite vacation spots in France. – Trans.

15 Cf. *Hérodote*'s special issue on historical geography (1994).

16 Lutetia is the original Gallic name of the village that became Paris. – Trans.

17 A play on the words *triste* (sad) and *bonne espérance* (hopefulness), itself a wordplay on the Cape of Good Hope (*Bonne Espérance* in French). – Trans.

18 '*Espace vécu*' is 'space perceived and practised by the people who live in it', J.-F. Staszak, 'Espace vécu', in J. Lévy and M. Lussault (eds), *Dictionnaire de la géographie et de l'espace des sociétés*, Paris, Belin, 2003, 341. It is distinct from 'lifeworld', defined by anglophone geographers as the spatio-temporal setting of everyday life. – Trans.

19 Cf. David Ley (ed.), *Humanistic Geography: Problems and Prospects. Place, Culture, Representation* (1983).

20 It would be more accurate to say 'along the lines of the model proposed by the North'. – Trans.

21 Cf. *La Planète des naufragés, essai sur l'après-développement* (1991).

22 Roots rather than foundation or basis: Bonnemaison favoured the word 'roots' rather than its abstract equivalents, and I have kept the term here and elsewhere in the text. – Trans.

23 Jean Monnet, a French politician, pioneered the concept of a unified Europe after World War II. – Trans.

24 André Cholley, *Guide de l'étudiant en géographie*, Paris, 1942.

25 Jean Tricart (1979) quoted in Pitte (1983, 15).

26 An allusion to tour package operators. – Trans.

27 S. C. Kolm, *Le Monde*, 18 April 1972.

28 Rue ('street') Saint-Jacques is in the heart of the Latin Quarter and therefore very familiar to students at the Geography Institute, where Bonnemaison taught. – Trans.

3 On whether culture and civilization are operational concepts in geography

1 Anthropic: anthropogenic; having to do with mankind. Today, the word is most commonly used in the expression 'anthropic principle'. Making not just life but intelligent life practically inevitable on Earth is called the anthropic principle. – Trans.

2 In this chapter Bonnemaison uses the term 'custom' (*la coutume*) in the singular, perhaps as a reminder of the word *kastom* used in Melanesia. *Kastom* is a key concept in Bonnemaison's work. – Trans.

3 Emile Benveniste, *Problèmes de linguistique générale*, Paris, Gallimard, 1966.

4 According to R. Gerard Ward and Darrell Tryon of the Australian National University, the paradox lies in the fact that Pacific Islanders can use their 'traditional' customs in order to win power and influence in the modern world (per. comm., 28 January 2003). – Trans.

5 A subtle way for Bonnemaison to defend his fieldwork in Tanna – and the geographic approach. For more light on Tanna's rebels, outside interests and the scientists who study them, see *The Tree and the Canoe* (1994). – Trans.

6 Before independence, the 'Condominium of the New Hebrides' was ruled jointly by Britain and France. – Trans.

7 Original words in English. – Trans.

8 In the central part of the island of Tanna. – Trans.

9 As originally defined, speciation is the formation of biological species or the processes leading to this end. Bonnemaison transferred the notion from biology to geography, using the concept of gradual divergence through space. (The formation of biological species may also occur abruptly by combination or transfer of genomes.) – Trans.

10 An allusion to the characters in the *Astérix* cartoon series, a perennial favourite in France since the 1960s. – Trans.

11 Original words in English. – Trans.

12 Édouard Herriot (1872–1957), writer, mayor of Lyons and politician, best-known for this famous quotation. He helped create the first mosque in Paris (1923). – Trans.

13 Cf. Gramsci's *Political Writings* (1974–83).

14 *La Révolution de l'An II* (July 1793 to July 1794), which in the midst of terror had set a day aside to celebrate the universal 'Supreme Being', ended with the downfall of Robespierre. – Trans.

15 One example of the French view of universal Truth is portrayed in Ken Alder, *The Measure of all Things: The Seven-Year Odyssey and Hidden Error that Transformed the World*, New York, Free Press, 2002. In 1792, the French National Assembly funded a survey of longitude by two French scientists. The goal was to devise a new standardized measurement system based on the metre as a portion of the longitudinal distance from pole to equator. The National Assembly wished to 'encompass nothing that was arbitrary, nor to the particular advantage of any people on the planet'. Today, the USA, Myanmar and Liberia are the only three nations in the world that do not officially employ the metric system. – Trans.

4 The cultural system

1 'In the United States about one-quarter of all prescriptions dispensed by pharmacies are substances extracted from plants. Another 13 per cent originate from micro-organisms and 3 per cent more from animals, for a total of about 40 per cent. [...] The commercial value of the relatively small number of natural products is substantial. [...] In spite of its obvious potential, however, only a tiny fraction of biodiversity has been utilized in medicine.' Edward O. Wilson, *The Future of Life,* New York, Alfred A. Knopf, 2002, 118–19. – Trans.

2 Cf. Jean-Robert Pitte's works on this theme.

3 These areas are also linguistic: *oc* was spoken in the south and *oïl* in the north. – Trans.

4 On this topic, see Augustin Berque, *Le Sauvage et l'artifice: les Japonais devant la nature* (1986).

5 From the Vanuatu pidgin *men ples*, a theme developed in *The Tree and the Canoe*. – Trans.

6 i.e. men who identify with a place. One of the key concepts of Tanna's culture. See *The Tree and the Canoe*, chapter 19. – Trans.

7 While *man ples* is a Bislama term widely used in Tanna, *man-tree* was coined by Bonnemaison. – Trans.

8 *Small men:* pidgin term, to be contrasted with Melanesian leaders or *big men*. – Trans.

9 *Kava* is a drug whose anxiolytic and hypnotic effects are currently being investigated by research laboratories in Europe and the USA. – Trans.

10 Here Bonnemaison used the plural: ethnogeographies. – Trans.

11 *Terroir*: see note 3 in Chapter 1. – Trans.

12 Rugby is mostly played in the southwest of France, where Bonnemaison spent his youth and had a house. – Trans.

13 The region around Paris. – Trans.

14 Grain sorghum. – Trans.

15 This sentence directed at students reminds the reader that the present text was originally delivered as a series of lectures at the Institute of Geography. – Trans.

16 Bonnemaison focused his professional attention on Melanesia rather than Polynesia or Micronesia, which may explain his statement that Melanesia is at the heart of the Pacific. The Polynesian triangle (Hawaii–New Zealand–Easter Island) occupies the geographical core of the Pacific. Which region is the leading force has been a matter of debate for some time among Pacific Islanders themselves. – Trans.

17 From the Greek *thalasso*, 'sea'. – Trans.

18 In 'The Ballad of East and West' (1889). The phrase is not as well-known in France as it is in English-speaking countries. – Trans.

19 Today we would say a digital or VR (virtual reality) culture. – Trans.

20 Original text in English. – Trans.

21 For instance, see R. Debray, *Les Diagonales du médiologue*, Paris, Éditions de la bibliothèque nationale de France, 2001. – Trans.

22 Lévi-Strauss coined the term 'cold societies'. – Trans.

23 *The American way of life*: original words in English. – Trans.

5 Conclusion: is the territory (or place) a new paradigm for human geography?

1 I am grateful to John Agnew who suggested the word 'place' as an alternative translation for '*territoire*'. Cf. John Agnew's introduction to the present edition, p. xvii. Although the two terms are analogous, they are not interchangeable. The term 'territory' is more aligned with Bonnemaison's ethnogeographic approach. With respect to the emotional link between people and place, Bonnemaison gave this connection the name of geographical feeling, which he describes in *The Tree and the Canoe*. – Trans.

2 The text of this chapter reproduces J. Bonnemaison's inaugural speech at a colloquium he organized with Luc Cambrézy in conjunction with University of Paris IV and ORSTOM/IRD, Paris, 1995. The colloquium was entitled 'Territory: A Link or a Frontier?', *Chroniques du Sud*, 18, ORSTOM (1996), 109–13. Also published in J. Bonnemaison, L. Cambrézy and L. Quinty-Bourgeois (eds), *Le Territoire, lien ou frontière?*, Paris, Éditions de l'ORSTOM, 1997, Collection colloques et séminaires, CD-ROM.

3 It is both an ante-world, in the sense of an earlier, anterior world, and an anti-world, in the sense of a rival or opposite world. Bonnemaison emphasized the latter here, but in his other writings he also discussed the former meaning. – Trans.

4 '*Il est idéel et même souvent idéal, alors que l'espace est matériel*'. With four words ending in 'l' the sentence is meant to rhyme, a good example of Bonnemaison's literary approach. – Trans.

5 '*La résonance entre l'homme et le monde*'.

6 Cf. Bruce Chatwin, *The Songlines*, London, Viking Penguin, 1987. – Trans.

7 'The blue crest line of the Vosges' was France's rallying cry in World War I. – Trans.

8 Cf. the Falklands War (1982) between the United Kingdom and Argentina. – Trans.

9 A lecturer in religion wrote these words about the link between place, negotiation and identity: 'Disagreement is at some level always about [another person's] location. It is about identity, about holding onto one's place in the family, in the neighborhood, bio-region, identified group, world. [...] [W]hen we argue, we need to remember that something about our place-identities is also on the line through the energies of communication. [...] [N]egotiators [from Bosnia/Serbia/Kosovo] would put their hands in their pockets just at the point of imminent resolution. One touched a rock from the motherland, another a small ziplock bag of dirt from his home country. Then things would fall apart. [...] The ancient monastics believed we all have rocks and soil in our pockets.' Barbara Patterson, 'The Rocks and Soil in our Pockets: Lessons on Conflict, Identity, and Place from Early Monastic Life,' *The Academic Exchange: An Online Place for Scholarly Conversation at Emory*, www.emory.edu/acad_exchange. Accessed 30 November 2002. – Trans.

10 Bonnemaison may be alluding to Michel Foucault's work here. – Trans.

Index

Page numbers in *italics* refer to illustrations.